What I Wish You Knew

H. J. Richardson

Copyright © 2023 H J Richardson

All rights reserved.

ISBN: 9798861809030

DEDICATION

For all the neurodivergent people who felt like everyone else got a rule book on how to be 'human' and for Little Harry, who never received her copy.

CONTENTS

	Acknowledgments	i
1	A Note from Little Harry	1
2	A Note from Big Harry	4
3	The Teddy Bear's Picnic	9
4	Something Called Autism	15
5	Cruella Deville & Lactose Intolerance	21
6	Things Get Worse Before They Get Better	27
7	Cherries, Webbed Toes & Raisin Fingers	33
8	The Colour Co-ordinated Caddy	49
9	Morrison's, Meltdowns & Bacon	65
10	Washing Machine Woes & The Start of Self-Advocacy	71

CONTENTS

11	Jacket Potatoes & General Nigmo Biffy	77
12	Infodumping with the Illustrator	87
13	The Hole in the Hedge	94
14	What Would a Diagnosis Mean for You?	108
15	The Mushroom Fiasco	114
16	Sensory Profiles & Stim Dancing	128
17	Horrid Henry & Hoovers	135
18	Power Poses & Presentations	148
19	An Onstage Accident	154
20	Without Words, I'm Still Heard	161

CONTENTS

21	Lucy's Silly Apples & A Giant Girl	166
22	'You Got This!'	179
23	My Alex & Basil	191
24	A Cockapoo & an Important Call	197
25	Gareth Gates & Bacon Croissants	204
26	An Author & a Bookworm	215
27	A Little, Orange Tile	220
28	Silent Strolls & Dickhead Detectors	227
29	The End of Harry	234
30	It Was In Front of Me All Along	238
31	What I Wish You Knew	243

ACKNOWLEDGMENTS

It has always been my dream to be an author, from the moment I first started to write. Words have been my biggest passion in life and have saved my life more times than I can count. I have to thank my parents for the unwavering support they have given me over the years, encouraging me to never give up on those dreams. My dad, who proofread and listened to my infodumps on countless phone calls. My mum, who without I would not be here today. My brother for teaching me it was enough to be myself and for making me the luckiest sister in the world, our distance in miles will never change our bond. My friends who have been such a big part of this book, you're all such wonderful, caring and hilarious people that have given me so much joy over the years. And finally, Jack, the most wonderful partner in life. He has taught me so many lessons, most of all how to love and accept myself for who I am. I feel lucky to be alive.

1
A NOTE FROM BIG HARRY

In January of 2022 I was diagnosed as autistic, at the age of twenty-six. That day was the start of a completely new life for me, learning who I was and what had happened to me as a result of being undiagnosed autistic and ADHD. Unpacking what the diagnoses meant started out with re-processing old memories of childhood where things now made sense. I started to write down these memories to process them and unpick them as I saw them now, as an informed adult. This led to the process of writing what is now in front of you.

So many tears have been shed writing this book, it has been a deeply personal but cathartic experience to explore my past and relate it to present day experiences. Being able to write my feelings and thoughts is a privilege that not every person has the luxury of and for that I feel grateful.

Words have always been the most important part of my life and I have used them in so many versions to tell my story and process the most difficult parts of my life, of which there have been many. I hope that my gift with words brings awareness, understanding and acceptance for many people who are blessed to spend time with wonderful neurodivergent people, like it has done for my own special people. It has been difficult to accept that I have experienced so many struggles all because I wasn't diagnosed, understood and supported for twenty-six years. However, I take comfort in that I can help to shape others' experiences by sharing my own so that those like me don't have to navigate the same battles.

I hope that my story highlights how important it is for neurodivergent children to understand their neurodivergent identity early, be informed of it and educated about it. I wish with everything that I have that my parents would have been able to sit down with me as a little girl and explain why I felt different to everyone else, talk to me about the support I might need and tell me not to internalise all of the things that I did. I wish that for my parents' sake, I could have had an earlier identification so that they could have at least some support in raising me and understanding me. I can't imagine the changes it would have made to all of our mental health.

As long as I can, I want to make sure young, neurodivergent children know that they don't have to change to make everyone else happy. We're different, but that doesn't make us worth any less, we have incredible things to bring to this world and as long as we mask those parts of ourselves, we will never fulfill our potential. Only now that I know about my identity have I finally been able to write my first book, something that I yearned for all of my life but without understanding of who I was I could never quite finish what I started. Only by embracing my differences have I been able to like who I am and love the parts of myself that I didn't allow myself to be.

I can accept now that I can't rewrite my own story with happy endings and earlier realisations, but with that maybe I can make a difference to others' lives and make that something they experience. I feel grateful that I've lived to bring a change to the world, no matter how small that change might be.

2
A NOTE FROM LITTLE HARRY

Before I begin the story, let me first introduce myself. I'm Harry, I'm eleven years old and I live with my mum and dad and my dog, Basil. I have three lots of grandparents, one in Spain (my dad's parents), one in England (my mum's parents) and one in Australia (my dad's birth mum). I've never actually met Grandma Australia, but I write to her, and I like that more than talking to someone anyway, she's really nice over letters but she might be a horror in real life (just like me).

I live in a little town in Yorkshire, it's very quiet and green and I love it! We live very close to grandma and grandpa England, they're only ten minutes from our house and I know that because I've timed it. Behind my house is my best friend Anna's house (a one-minute walk up the garden and over the wall that separates our houses or a five-minute walk up Den Lane if you have to go to the front door). Down the road is my friend Linda's house (eleven minutes away), the tennis club is the opposite direction, which is six minutes from my house and my school is a bit further than that at twenty-one minutes away. Next door to us on the right is an old lady called Beth, who has two dogs Barky and Teddy, sometimes she lets me walk them for some spending money. On the other side is another old lady called Karen and she has a tortoise; she's also got something called dementia and I don't like talking to her because she surprises me when she comes out of her hedge and asks me the same questions when I've already answered them.

My brother comes to stay some weekends because he has a different mum to me, he's called a half-brother, but I don't like that, so I just call him my brother or 'my Alex' because that's what he is. Anyway, he's more than half a person, he's my favourite ever person, so maybe he's a whole person and a half!

I call the tennis club my second home and I know everyone's number plates and what cars they have. I like that because when we arrive I know who I will see so I can quickly think what I want to say to them. At the tennis club we have seven outdoor courts and four indoor courts. There's also a gym, a café and a few practice spaces. I like it when mum and dad park their car in exactly the same spots because it unsettles me if they don't.

Here are a few things you should know about me before you read on:

- I'm autistic but I don't know that until I'm very old, twenty-six whole years old (ancient!). Instead, I got given lots of other labels like 'depression' and 'anxiety' that were caused by people not understanding and supporting my brain.
- I also have Attention Deficit Hyperactivity Disorder (ADHD) that hasn't been diagnosed yet even when I'm an adult. This means that I struggle with a lot of 'executive function' tasks like initiation, planning, organisation, time management and lots more. It means that even as an adult I rely

a lot on my parents and other people to help me do things like booking appointments. It can be really frustrating.

- It is very likely that I struggle with something called demand avoidance that like my autism was never really understood. Demand avoidance makes it really difficult for me to do things other people ask me to do when they word it in certain ways or in a certain tone. It's sometimes like my brain won't let me do the things people ask me to do even when I really want to do it, just to make them happy.
- I have sensory processing difficulties that I don't really understand until I'm older. My sensory difficulties are related to my autism that means I have sensitivities to certain sounds, sights and touch. If I have too much of these things I get migraines, stomachaches and sensory overload, which makes me have meltdowns or shutdowns. Because of my sensory difficulties I also have a very restricted diet and feel physically sick if I have to eat certain textures or tastes and sometimes, I'll even go off things I really liked before because they start to taste wrong. Everyone thinks I'm really fussy but I'm not trying to be difficult.
- I'm also semi-speaking, which means sometimes I can't, or find it exhausting to speak. Sometimes I have to use AAC (Alternative & Augmentative Communication) which is different ways of communicating other than speech. People don't understand this and often force me to speak, which feels horrible!
- I am lactose intolerant, which the doctors found out when I was tiny, specifically when my mum stopped breast feeding me and so I got poorly very often and I had lots of people around me worried and stressed, which made me upset.

- Unlike some autistic people, I walked and talked and rode a bike so much earlier than all the kids my age. I was super clever at school from being tiny and read books all the time, so I was really good with words. I've also always had great hand-eye-coordination and can do any sport I try, apart from football and dancing because my feet don't coordinate well with the rest of my body. This is called motor planning and lots of autistic people struggle with it. I suppose this made it more difficult for my autism to get diagnosed because lots of doctors think people aren't autistic if they are coordinated and articulate.

All this is making me think that doctors are a bit rubbish because me and mum always go to the doctors and try to ask for some help, but we just get told we are being silly. But now I write down all those things above, I think that the doctors were the only silly sausages. Doctors say 'people with autism' and not autistic people and I don't like that because it's separate from me, but autism is part of who I am, even though I don't know it yet. People only use person-first language when they talk about negative medical things that can harm you, like person with cancer or person with diabetes.

Medical professionals say I have 'Autism Spectrum Disorder', which is characterised by 'impairments' in social skills and verbal and non-verbal communication, with 'symptoms' like repetitive behaviours. I think the language they use is silly because for me, autism is a difference not a disorder, I don't understand why people try to change people like me to be 'normal' with 'intervention' and 'treatment.' Why can't we just be the way that we are? Every autistic person is very different, just like everyone else in the world is unique and different from each other. Often people make up silly stereotypes about us like that we have no emotions or that it's only boys that are autistic. I wish people would learn a bit more about autism so that they could be respectful and kind to us all and just accept us for who we are.

Because of my ADHD, my brain works differently from lots of other people, I often think about lots of different things at once and go off track a lot, so this book has lots of different parts of it that I would like to explain. I have written about my experiences as little Harry, followed by my experiences as Big Harry. This is because, when I get older and discover my autistic identity, I start to do lots of thinking about little Harry's memories and how I might see them in a very different way when I know what is different about my brain. I'm always feeling very upset with myself and shameful that I make everyone cross and I'm such hard work, but my diagnosis makes big me feel okay about all those things because I am always just misunderstood.

So, here's my story…

3
THE TEDDY BEAR'S PICNIC

2000

Today is the teddy bear's picnic and I'm so excited to take Scruffy and show him my school. Scruffy has to wait for me all day at home and I'm sure he gets very bored in my purple bedroom that I wish was blue (but I can't have because girls' bedrooms aren't blue!). I really miss him while I'm at school, he makes me feel safe and happy and he's my favourite ever teddy. Daddy says he was one of my first teddies and he was a present from mummy's friend Susan, I wish he was my first teddy because he means the most to me. We call him Scruffy because he has brown, shaggy fur and looks a little bit sad. He's got patchwork ears, hands and feet and a little tail that's a bit matted. He's a lovely rabbit and has a tag around his neck that says 'Scruffy' because I made mummy write it on there. Scruffy is far better than anyone else's teddies and I can't wait to see how jealous everyone is going to be of him, especially Grace, she's going to think I'm so cool with Scruffy at the picnic. Grace is a girl in my class, one of the only girls and I really want to be friends with her and Maisie, but they're always really mean to me. Whenever I try to join in with what they're playing with they shoo me away and tell me I'm annoying. I keep trying to be more like them but I'm always different, I always end up making a mistake and they ask me to go away.

This morning, I'm sat in the kitchen, up at the table with one of my legs tucked under my bum and the other dangling down. I always get told off when I sit like this, but I try hiding it under the table, it's horrible if I sit like everyone else, I can't concentrate. I can hear mummy coming downstairs so I reassemble my position under the table, two legs dangling down, before she gets chance to remind me. As she enters the kitchen, she greets me with a tired 'good morning, sweetheart' and orders me to finish my breakfast quickly before we leave. She busies herself brushing through her straight, blond hair and adding lipstick to her already full lips. Mummy looks nothing like me in most ways, especially her height, which she used to her advantage as a star basketball player. Instead, everyone says I look the spitting image of daddy, a smatter of freckles across my nose, sticky-out ears and a mass of auburn hair. I even have daddy's sense of humour and a mischievous streak that we both get away with using our cheeky smiles. Mummy calls it my 'wide-mouth frog' smile because it's so wide and hides a multitude of sins, as soon as they see the grin, they forget what I've done wrong and laugh with me. As she finishes making herself even more beautiful, she turns her attention on me and casts her eyes over the table, they pass over Scruffy next to my green and yellow school bag.

"Harry you can't take Scruffy to school." She looks at me apologetically and smiles warmly, "why don't I go and get Snowy for you and we can put her in a pretty dress for the Teddy Bear's Picnic?"

"No, Scruffy has to come with me. He's been looking

forward to it all week and he can't wait to see school." I beam back at her.

"Harry, you know how forgetful you are! You'd be so upset if you lost Scruffy at school. Also don't you think it would be nicer to take Snowy? She's much cleaner and I'm sure all the girls will love her." Mum knows how much I want to and try to be friends with the girls, she sits with me every night as I talk to her about what went wrong with them that day and what we can do tomorrow to make things better. Maybe she's right, the girls might like Snowy better, but I don't want Snowy, I love her but she's not Scruffy and she never will be. Snowy is a white rabbit with little pink bits in her ears, a cute, friendly face and a little ribbon around her neck. She has lots of different dresses, but I don't like dresses, so I can't understand why Snowy would want to wear them. I like dressing her up in shorts and t-shirts just like me, dresses are silly, and my legs get all cold in them, plus mummy says I have to sit in a different way when I wear dresses and I don't like that. I'm pretty sure Snowy doesn't get told to sit a different way in her dresses; maybe that's why she's always so smiley.

Sometimes, when I look at Snowy, she reminds me of what I should look and behave like, like everyone keeps telling me. But I'm not like her; no matter how much I try I'm just like Scruffy and no one seems to like him that much. Everyone prefers Snowy with her pretty dresses, clean fur and smiley face. I think Scruffy has more character, he's different and I like different things.

"Okay, I'll take them both." I announce, proud that I have compromised. Scruffy and Snowy are a pair, they're the best of friends but Snowy knows she'll never be my favourite and she's okay with that. I like playing with them, especially with daddy, he often puts on shows for me with all my teddies (I have a lot) and will make Snowy and Scruffy talk to me to tell me it's time for bed and makes them climb all the way up the stairs to bed with me, where he tucks me in with them either side of me every night. Daddy knows that he has to give all three of us kisses on the forehead before sleep otherwise we won't sleep.

I look back at mum with upset eyes. Apparently, Mrs Howell says only one teddy can come to the picnic and mummy says that has to be Snowy, I try to get daddy to change her mind, but he agrees that I would only leave Scruffy at school and be upset. They're wrong, I would never leave him there, he's my very favourite but I know I'm not going to change their minds, mum has decided and when she says 'no' she means it. Begrudgingly, I eat my breakfast, collect my things and follow mum into our car.

Right now, as we drive to school, I don't like Snowy, every time I look at her, she makes me more and more angry and as we get closer to school I start to feel really hot, something that always happens when I'm about to either explode or implode.

As the hot feeling rises, I realise I haven't spoken a word to mummy since daddy left for work, which is a while ago now, I think. When I get upset, I don't feel like I can talk and everyone tries to get me to speak and I don't like it. It hurts my brain to use words when I don't feel okay, sometimes the words come out all wrong and sometimes they don't come out at all, and I have to wrap a blanket over my head or run away. Now that I've had time to process how mean and unfair everyone has been this morning, I feel really cross, silly Snowy for being a teddy that other people like more than Scruffy; silly mummy for making me take the wrong teddy to school; silly daddy for agreeing with her; silly Mrs Howell for making silly rules and silly Teddy Bear's picnic. I start to cry silently as we approach school because I'm starting to feel all wobbly, like I might scream and run away from everyone. No one seems to understand that I had a plan in my head of exactly what my day was going to look like and that involved Scruffy being at school with me and now that plan has changed, and I hate it when that happens. Now I'm confused and scared about what my day is going to look like, so I don't want to go to school.

I usually like school but because of what's happened this morning it doesn't feel safe. I know I will have to hide my feelings whilst I'm there and I'm not sure I can do that today. I can't scream at school, I can't kick and hit and run away from everyone. I can't even hide and be quiet like I want to be. I'm so scared, I want to hide in the footwell of the car, and I want everyone but mummy and daddy and Scruffy to be away from me. I just want quiet and dark and safety. I really, really don't want to go to school but I can't use my words right now so I just clutch Snowy tight, pretending she's shaggy and brown and it doesn't matter anyway because my tears are blurring up everything so I can't see her. Suddenly, mummy stops the car as we pull up to the school gates; she leans over to where I'm sat in the passenger seat and places her hand on my hair, smoothing it down.

"You'll be okay." She says gently as she continues to stroke my hair. I don't want my head to be touched, it makes my insides hurt so I move away but then I feel bad when I realise that might have upset her. We get out of the car without me saying a word and walk to the front gates, everyone is there with their favourite teddies, all clean and in pretty clothes and bows, just like Snowy. I don't want my teddy to be like the rest of them, he's so much better because he's different. It makes me even more scared of going to school seeing all their teddies, it's just not right, no one usually has a teddy with them, I don't like it.

Mummy turns to give me a kiss before she leaves, and I just want to tell her that I want her to stay and for her to take me home and wrap me up in my blanket and be safe and away from all these scary teddies. I spot Joseph as I anxiously scan the crowd of children, he has a teddy with an angry face and I can't look away from it, I'm starting to feel even hotter, too hot now. But still the words won't come, and I turn away from mummy, even though all I want is a big hug and for her not to leave. She takes that as a sign that I'm still angry and I watch her walk away, tears stream silently down my face, which I wipe away with Snowy's pink ear. It's time to put the mask on now and be the good little   girl   I   always   am   at   school.

4
SOMETHING CALLED AUTISM

January 2022

"How are you feeling about it all? What do you think she's going to say?" My dad asks on the phone as I drive home from work. Today is the day that I find out my autism assessment results from Dr Hudson.

"Well, I don't understand how she can't not give me the diagnosis, I'm so very clearly autistic, I meet so much of the criteria. I think I'm just really scared she won't give me the diagnosis because I've started to finally understand myself and accept that everything wasn't my fault." Tears prick my eyes at the thought of going back to the drawing board to figure out why I've always felt different.

"It's okay, whatever the outcome we'll figure it out together." He reassures me, "Good luck, sweetheart and give us a call to let us know what she says."

"Will do!" I end the phone call with tears filling my eyes and a heavy load of anxiety in my stomach. I'm sure I'll get the diagnosis tonight and my life will change, and everything will make sense, but I'm still going to panic. There's that small chance that she'll tell me I'm not autistic and then I don't know where to go from there, I know in my gut that this is what I've been waiting for my whole life.

* * *

"So, how are you feeling?" Dr Hudson asks me as I answer her call with a wide grin.

"I'm extremely nervous, but also excited I think." I smile, realising I'm talking at quite a pace and try to slow myself down. "Anxious anticipation I think?"

"Would you like me to go through things first or would you like me to get straight into your results?"

"Straight to the results!" I say without thought.

"That's what I thought," she grins, "well I can confirm you meet the diagnostic criteria for autism." And that's all I need to know, I grin from ear to ear, it all makes so much sense, everything I've felt all of my life makes so much sense now. I breathe out; apparently, I'd been holding my breath this entire time.

All of the times I had felt unable to fit in with everyone else, to conform to a rule book that everyone else seemed to have, unable to make my needs known. The feeling of confirmation is intense, it's like a piece of me that has been missing forever finally slots into place and everything feels complete. Dr Hudson is still talking, and I zone back into the conversation.

"So, lots of people have different preferences for their autistic identity, some people describe themselves as an 'autistic person', some a 'person with autism'. Do you have thoughts on what you'd be most comfortable with? You may not have thought about this yet."

"Oh I definitely have!" I smile, "I'm autistic." The words feel so right on my lips, and I can't help but boast a wider grin.

"That's wonderful, I'm so happy you have found so much positivity in your identity so quickly. There will be a lot to process and work through now you've had your diagnosis, but this is a very positive first step and I'm here to help you along the way, should you wish me too." Dr Hudson describes the report she will send me and what I should do now I've had my diagnosis, including a strong emphasis on finding my community and sharing experiences. Her words fly past my ears as I struggle to remain focused on the conversation, there's lots of information to take in and I'm focused on just one aspect, I am autistic, it's confirmed. I can't wait to speak to my family and friends and talk it all through with them, I feel like I have so much to say. I become aware of the feeling inside me, it's a wonderful feeling that runs all the way from my head to my toes, it's warm and sparkly and I would like to name it elation, at least that's what I think it is, I'm not sure I've experienced so much of it for such a prolonged period of time. The only times I've felt it before are when I've felt immensely close to another person, on my graduation, when I won tennis and golf tournaments and when I took Meeno, my dog home. There really aren't any words to describe my thoughts and my feelings, it's like a rainbow shower of positive emotion and I want to stay in it for as long as I can. Dr Hudson waves goodbye to me on the screen and I'm unable to recount what her words have been for the past five minutes, it's all noise compared with the whizzing thoughts in my head.

I continue to sit at the desk; long after the call has ended. I keep repeating the words out loud *'I'm autistic, I'm autistic, I'm autistic'*. It's like a chant that I'm using to get used to the new words on my lips; maybe I'm making up for lost time. It's not that now I am autistic, I have always been, but I had no idea until today. It feels like my life has only just started because up until now I'd been living under the wrong identity. I was missing one of the most fundamental parts of me, buried so deep down that no one could see it, until now. There's an intense feeling of freedom as I close my laptop, gather my things and shut the door of the study, leaving behind a room of new discovery.

*   *   *

That night, I lay awake having talked the diagnosis over with my parents and my boyfriend, Jack. No amount of talking about it will ever feel enough and so I lay wide awake unable to sleep, unable to think about anything else or relax into unconsciousness. All of these years I've felt like I'm wrong and broken, all to now be described within one word: *autism*. All of the times I've felt misunderstood, judged, misinterpreted, scared, lonely, it all makes sense now there's a word to put the pieces together: *autism*. I run my mind over conversations that I'm going to have in my head and how I will tell people about my life-changing news, will they be as excited as I am? Will they understand me better? I briefly wonder if I will lose friendships because they won't understand or maybe when I start to unmask, we won't be as compatible anymore, this feeling sits okay with me, I have to put myself first now. Dr Hudson's words run through my head: "you've changed yourself to fit everyone else your whole life, now it's time for everyone else to adapt to support you."

I wonder about what my life would have been had the diagnosis come sooner but I try to cast that thought aside, there's no point dwelling on what could have been and anyways I wouldn't be who I am today without the experiences I've had. I shudder and pull Scruffy closer as I think about the times I was at crisis point in my life, desperate for a lifeline, an answer and someone to give me a word like *autism*. Would I have accepted it? Or would I have rejected it just like I did depression and anxiety? Would it have saved me all of the suffering I experienced? Would I be a better person? There are so many questions I feel are unanswered and will never be answered and a hollow feeling enters my core.

I consider the times I felt like an alien, like everyone else around me spoke a different language and moved in unfamiliar ways. I knew how different I was from so little, and I did everything I could to plug the gaps so that no one would notice but somehow, they always did. There are many people who have loved me and continue to love me in my life despite and because of those differences, to some I am new and exciting and different. I wish everyone had seen me that way, I wish I hadn't felt the need to dispel the different parts of me, like my inability to wear pink and girlie clothes. I wish I hadn't caved to society's expectation of what a woman should look and behave like, I wish I could have just been a bit more me.

My big brother, Alex enters my mind and I bite my lip as emotions surge. I want so badly to reach for my phone and drop him a text telling him the news and to call me as soon as he can, but I know that he's away right now and out of reach. He will text me back when he gets signal, I don't need to pester him. If anyone taught me that it was okay to be myself, it was my brother. He always told me I was being silly when I tried to be like the other girls, and he loved me for my boyish ways, unique humour and annoying habits. I wish I could have loved myself the way I was, just as my brother had.

Will anyone ever understand what it feels like to be identified as autistic this way? When you're twenty-six and seem to have everything on the surface, the career, boyfriend, the family, the house. To everyone on the outside looking in, I appear like I've got it all figured out but I'm not anywhere near, I've been living a lie and all the things around me don't feel like they're mine anymore. This duvet, did I pick this out? I suddenly realise I don't like the bedding that surrounds my body. Did I make the decision to buy this or was I supported by my parents to make this decision, just like everything else?

How did I get here? I realise in this moment that I don't know how much of the life I live is for myself and which parts of it are for appearances and to make everyone else happy. How genuine is this life I've built around me? Panic sets in as I look over to Jack, silently sleeping, does the unmasked version of my life feature him? I suddenly feel suffocated by this strange realisation that I've made barely any decision so far in my life, I've had no autonomy of my life, I've passed every decision I've ever made through other people. What if those people don't actually know what is right or good for me?

These thoughts stay with me until around two thirty, when I slip into a well needed, deep sleep.

5
CRUELLA DEVILLE & LACTOSE INTOLERANCE

2005

Mum is angry again. We're driving to school in her red, Ford Fiesta that I call Biffa. She's driving like Cruella Deville, quick, jolting movements that she always does when she's annoyed. I'm trying to eat my breakfast, but the bottom of the chocolate chip muffin is dry and it feels all wrong in my mouth. The top of the muffin was better but still not okay; it stuck to the roof of my mouth and makes me feel sick. I retch a little and hope mummy won't notice, but she sees everything. The muffin is too big; I can't eat it all today.

"I feel sick." I mutter, attempting to hide how much of the muffin is left. Mum is holding her breath and she's gone all red in the face, I know she's trying to compose herself. I feel bad, I know how unhappy it makes her when I don't eat my breakfast and she's told me so many times that she's worried about my weight. I'm a tiny, little thing; big blue eyes that change colour in the light, from green to grey to blue. I'm often likened to a little pixie, with my freckles, slightness and cheeky smile, not to mention my Dumbo ears. The most prominent thing about me is my auburn hair, ringlets and masses of it, so much so that mummy had to cut me a fringe to help it stop getting so knotted. I don't like the fringe, it rests of my forehead, and I don't like the feel of things on my face, it makes me feel all itchy.

"Harry, I've tried everything." Mum snaps, "you've had chocolate croissants, crumpets, coco pops, hot cross buns, iced buns and now you won't eat any of them, not even chocolate buns." I pick out the chocolate chips from the remainder of the muffin, hoping it will distract her from what's left of it. The rest of it falls apart in my fingers and I start to feel sicker at the thought of it touching my tongue.

"I don't know what else to give you." She continues, "I need you to eat. I just really need you to eat something." There are tears in her eyes now and she pulls Biffa over in a lay-by just before the steep hill to school. She doesn't turn off the engine, just sits there staring ahead, in thought. Mum says when I was really little, they couldn't find nappies to fit me because I lost so much weight, apparently I dropped off the charts they had in the doctors that compares children's healthy and unhealthy weights. There were times when I really wouldn't eat anything, and mum and dad would have to feed me individual vegetables in the mouths of my toy dinosaurs. Instead of a knife and fork I had a triceratops and a brontosaurus, it makes me laugh thinking of the dinosaurs with peas and carrots in their mouths. Dad said the only time I would eat was if my dinosaurs collected the food off the plate and fed me, because I was obsessed with dinosaurs until Charlotte, a girl in the year above me in school, told me they weren't cool.

Then I had to hide my love for all things dinosaur.

Mum always looks really worried when she talks about my eating and that makes me feel all stressed, just like when my hair touches my face. I have something called lactose intolerance, which means I can't eat milk or dairy products, which is fine by me because milk is yucky. Mum and dad tried to get me to eat a substitute for milk called Soya Milk; I think it was the yuckiest thing I've ever tasted. The doctors told them I was getting really ill, and everyone was worried I wasn't getting enough calcium, which is something in milk. They made my parents get this yucky milk and put it on my cereal. I kept telling them it was not okay, and it was yucky, but they wouldn't listen, they just shouted at me when I started gipping and said I was being dramatic. I tried to make them understand that the cereal was all soggy and that made me feel sick and all nasty inside my mouth and that I couldn't swallow it. I think the doctors who told mummy and daddy I had to eat it were really mean because I had to sit at the table until I'd eaten it all and I kept having to sneak to the bathroom to spit it out whenever they left the room. I don't know how much was milk in my cereal and how much of it was the water from my eyes but it felt a lot of liquid. Making me eat cereal with milk on it didn't last very long, dad said to mum it wasn't worth the tantrums and tears when he thought I wasn't listening. I look back at the bun in my hand; if I just persevere with telling mum it's making me feel sick maybe she'll give in like she did with the milky cereal.

"I just can't eat anymore, I'm sorry mum. It's all dry and tastes funny in my mouth. I'll try something else." I offer, trying to make her feel okay again.

"I just don't know what to give you, Harry. You seem to like things for a while and then you go off them so quickly. I've had to throw so much food away or put things in the freezer because you just go off it immediately and

I've gone and bought another week's worth of it."

"It just tastes yucky sometimes." I complain, why does she not understand what I mean? No one seems to have the same problem; maybe it's only me in the world. "I'll have crumpets tomorrow." I smile, feeling triumphant that I've solved her problem.

"What?" She turns to me, obviously shocked. "Only last week you claimed crumpets were too soft and yucky and threw them in the bin! And now, now you'll eat them again?"

"Well they were yucky." I explain, why does she not understand this? "I think I'd like them now though."

"I just don't get it." She sighs and turns the steering wheel, pulling back out of the lay-by and down the hill to school.

Everyone says my school is really small, but to me there's lots of people, seventy-five Mrs Howell says, which is lots! Sometimes we have to sit in the main room for assembly and there's so many people that the teachers have to stand round the edges of the room, and it makes me feel all squishy and hot. I feel hot a lot and when I feel hot, my head gets all warm and I can't think quickly and then I get angry and need to move away from everyone and get out of my clothes.

My school, Sunflowers, is an old house and there are six classrooms, from nursery to year five, year fives and sixes learn together in one big classroom at the top of the school. That's where my class is, year six. Our teacher is Mrs Howell, she's an amazing teacher and I'm learning lots, but my favourite teacher was Mrs Betties, she let me be me, I could write how I like where my fingers are comfortable and don't hurt, take breaks to go to the toilet often and she didn't tell me off for making what everyone else calls 'silly mistakes'. Mrs Howell is good too, she tells me that I'm a very good writer and last year she put one of my essays up on the wall because it was so good, it was about an enchanted forest with moss-encrusted stones and dappled sunlight, all things I'd read in my favourite books. Mrs Howell helps us learn new words, which she writes on the board at the start of each week, and I really like them because I get to use new words in my writing. We have a spelling test on the words at the end of each week and I always get them all right. I like being good at my work because people tell me how great I am doing and often I don't feel like I am very good at things because the other people laugh at me and point out my mistakes.

We often have to read out loud in class and some of the other kids annoy me because they get the words wrong and don't read it with any changes in their voice, so I get bored and stressed. I'm a good reader, so Mrs Howell says at parents' evening, although sometimes I get all confused about where I am in the book and need to use my finger or a ruler to keep track of where I am. A lot of the time, I miss out little words in the book because my eyes are reading the words faster than my mouth can speak them and this makes me really annoyed because people tell me to go back over the words and read them properly, but I already know what the words say. I love books and I like to play games with the same stories after I've finished them because I don't like the books being finished and I enjoy feeling like I'm other people in different worlds. A lot of the time, I pretend to be different people in books that I like, like the main girl characters who are strong and brave and confident. I don't feel confident, everyone says I'm very shy and I don't like to talk to people who I don't know or in places I've never been. At school, I pretend that I'm the popular girl and everyone likes me, and I even change my name in my head to help me pretend. Sometimes, when I'm not feeling confident and I feel overwhelmed, I will go to the toilet for a bit and sit with the toilet seat down trying to get back into character, thinking what the main character in my book would think, say and do.

When I'm in different characters people like me more and people don't laugh at me as much. I like pretending that I'm confident because then I don't feel so scared of everything and everyone. I told mummy that a lot of the time it feels like I have a mask on, and people don't really get to see who I am without it. Mum asked me lots of questions about my mask, she asked me what it looks like and I couldn't tell her.

"It looks like me, mum." I said, "I just pretend to be what everyone wants to me to look and act like because lots of the time if I don't wear my mask people are mean to me." I don't think she really understood what I meant; she doesn't always believe me when I say I'm being bullied because the kids who are mean are really nice to me when adults are around. She also asked me what it feels like, and I told her that wearing my mask makes me really tired and when I've been using it for too long, I get really tired and it's hard to use words so I just want to be quiet and sit in the dark on my own for a while. A lot of the time words feel really hard to use especially when I'm too tired to wear my mask, but lots of people get angry with me when I don't talk. Adults tell me I'm being rude and I'm not, I'm trying so hard to talk really but sometimes I can't and they don't like it when I point to things to ask for their help.

At the moment my mask is Harriet the Spy, she's cool and funny and is always very organised. I'm not organised, I always get told off for having the wrong things and forgetting to do things, especially at home. When I'm at school, I pretend I'm Harriet the Spy, with my backpack of spy gear and a notebook to write everything down and everyone seems to like the jokes I tell that Harriet used. I make sure every morning I have all my pens and pencils in my pencil case and my books, because that is what Harriet the Spy would do.

WHAT I WISH YOU KNEW

When I was Hermione Granger from Harry Potter, everyone rolled their eyes because I kept putting my hand up in class and always answering correctly, so I stopped doing that because no one seemed to like the Hermione Granger version of Harry in school. Harriet the Spy people seemed to like though, people like me more when I'm organised, polite and attentive, so Harriet the Spy I will continue to be until I find an even better character.

6
THINGS GET WORSE BEFORE THEY GET BETTER

May 2022

I slump down the side of the bed, facing the floor length mirror. The shower has left mottled red splashes on my legs and my wet hair sticks to my head and face. All of a sudden, I realise that this is going to be it for a while, I'm stuck here now with no motivation to walk the dog, tidy my clothes away or do anything else that was on my task list. A vacant stare starts, and I completely zone out for the environment and my internal feelings, dissociation looms.

I don't know how long I'm in this state, but I begin to have awareness that I'm staring at myself in the mirror. My eyes connect with those in the reflection, but I don't recognise them, they're dull and lifeless and none of the body looking back at me moves or shows any sign of life. *Is this what I look like? Is this me? Am I alive?* Slowly, my mind becomes aware of its environment, I don't feel anything around me but internally there's a suffocating feeling of emptiness. I feel like I did eight years ago, in my first year of university, sat in my bed with complete numbness for hours without the ability to move or have conscious thought. I feel trapped and I start to panic, still the face staring back at me shows no sign of life, despite the internal chaos. *How did I get here?*

Meeno, my apricot-coloured Cockapoo puppy, pushes open the bedroom door with his paws and strides into the room, nudging my face with his little, wet nose. It brings me out of the stare, the emptiness and feeling begins to connect to the side of my face his nose made contact with. Without warning, tears burst out of my eyes, and I collapse into external release, all the feelings explode out of me like a ripe tomato bursts when the knife cuts its surface. I knew that I was carrying a lot, but I didn't realise the depth of the emotions that have been suppressed within the furthest corners of my body. The tears don't stop; Meeno mops them up as best as he can with his tongue, catching the specks as they fall from my eyes. He shuffles closer as I sob and his tiny, fluffy paw rests of my arm, soothing me.

"I don't want you to go to mum and dad's tonight, Meeno." I whisper to him, a set of new tears bursting from my eyes. Tonight, my parents are looking after him for me. "When you go, I'll be alone and I'm always alone when you're not here." Of course, I'm not alone physically, Jack is at home too but when I feel like this there is no human contact that makes me feel heard or alive, only the love of my dog. He looks back at me with loving eyes and starts to lick my fingers.

Breaking the trance-like state, my body shifts from its paralysed position and I find my feet, slowly and carefully, gripping the edge of the bed to support my body weight. I'm dizzy as I clutch the end of the bed, Meeno winds himself through my legs to let me know he's still there.

As my focus comes back to the room, I become aware of Jack downstairs, singing with his headphones in and the sound breaks a wave of anger that rises from my core all the way to my head, not allowing me to have any thoughts other than panic. I need to stop hearing that sound, it's too much, it's taking over my whole body and I want to scream to drown it out. Instead, I slam the door shut and retreat into silence again whilst I tidy my clothes away.

As I fold Jack's t-shirts, I hear his footsteps on the stairs and my shoulders stiffen, I'm not ready for people, not Jack, not anyone, I need to be away from any noise, interruption and interaction. He enters the room and I turn my back, unable to look at him and have him look at me, the thought of being looked at sends shivers down my spine and my fingernails embed themselves into my palms. *Stop! Stop! Stop!* But he doesn't hear my silent pleas for him to leave me alone; he doesn't stop encroaching on my private space. His singing approaches, his body inches from mine, it's too much. I break free of the claustrophobia, shoving past him to escape the room. He offers out his arms to me and I reject them, turning my head away and cramming myself into the furthest corner of the room, my eyes covered by the palms of my hands.

"Can I have a hug?" He says, directing his question at my vulnerable and unconcealable face. Last week, I asked him to ask me for a hug before he touches me because at the minute physical touch is just too much for me to cope with. I shake my head in response to his question and attempt to move further away, he moves further towards me in response. "A high-five? An elbow?" Again, I shake my head and as he nears once again, I run for the hallway and slam the door, escaping from the proximity of his touch. I hear Meeno jumping on the bed and run back into the room to remove him from the neatly made sheets.

"Get off!" I yell at the bewildered dog and turn to Jack, all of my anger now redirected. "Stop winding him up! Whenever he's around you he goes wild and starts jumping on things. Just stop!"

"Are you seriously blaming me for this?" He looks puzzled, I'm not really, I just want to scream at him to get away from me and stop smothering me, even though he hasn't even touched me. That's what I want to yell, but I don't, and he continues, "It's clear you're upset about something and it's nothing to do with me, you can apologise to me later when I get home."

"Go away!" I yell after him as he leaves the room. To the outside eye, I look angry but inside I'm scared, and my heart is sinking. I'm like a caged animal that can't escape and so it bites from fear. Inside I'm completely falling apart, my brain isn't working, words aren't properly accessible, and my sensory system is on fire. I can't explain that to him, there are no words. I can't explain that I just need him to sit in the same room, at the furthest end from me as possible and just be there whilst I cry. I need him to look away from me but be there. I want him to touch my hand without touching it. I want everything and nothing from him at the same time and my head just *hurts,* it *burns* from the thoughts. I can't figure out what will help me in this situation and so I push everyone and everything away from me because that's safer. I'm completely out of control and it's bloody scary, my insides feel like they're melting. I have no words to explain the inner turmoil, but still, it only looks like anger.

Jack closes the door after him and tears explode from me, my breathing heaves heavy, in and out at a rapid pace. I'm unable to get ample air into my lungs and I just want to crawl into the smallest space possible and hide away from the world without anyone and anything but Meeno. It's suffocating how much I want to run after Jack, pull him inside and just rest my weight on him, but I can't. My body won't move, and my mind won't allow me to concede, as much as I will it to. I think of my parents and how much I want them to be here so I can completely break down and have them tell me it's going to be okay when it really feels like it won't.

I have an overwhelming urge to hit my hands against my head and thump my whole body because I can't escape from this tidal wave of feeling that intensifies with each inhalation. My mind spins to the week ahead, my birthday and all the plans Jack has made for us in Edinburgh, instead of excitement I feel overwhelmed. I just want to run out of the house and hide away from it all, all of the obligations and pressure. I can't cope with disappointing him if I can't be me whilst we're away. Worry sets in and I start to anxiously ponder what he will feel if I'm a shell of myself, will he regret all the wasted effort he will have gone to? Will he start to question if we have a future? I fight the urge to tell him I'm moving back in with my parents, out of our home, because I can't face the rejection if he was to tell me he can't love this part of me. I just can't cope with being what everyone else needs me to be, it's easier not to show my most vulnerable parts because everyone runs away in the end.

I'm trying so hard, still, even after knowing all the damage it has done, to mask and make everyone else feel comfortable even though there's this internal war zone going on in my body, my mind and my bones. I just want to be away from *everything*. The more I think of the events I've committed to the more I start to panic, our holidays to Wales and Bali with Jack's family, an Ed Sheeran concert next month, my birthday celebrations, work, my presentation in front of a hundred-odd people, going to visit my brother. All I really want to do is go and hide away in a forest in a hut with Meeno, where I can focus on my mind and process all of the sacramental trauma that has embedded itself in my core. The unresolved emotions that burn within me, a product of being alienated, ostracised, critisised, abused by misdiagnoses, misunderstandings, miscommunications, mistreatment. The trauma of being neurodivergent is so profound and once again, I sink to the bedroom floor feeling more broken than I've ever felt. Not broken because I'm faulty but because the world has let me down so many times, it's spat me out and shaped me into someone I can no longer recognise and continue to be, and I don't know where I can go from here.

I realise in this moment, as I curl into a ball on the carpet in a puddle of tears that this is going to take some time to figure out. There's so much internal damage rooted in me that I was never aware of and that no one who hasn't experienced a late diagnosis will ever understand. I need to work through my trauma and from what I've seen; things get a whole lot worse before they start to get better. This is reality now; this is what I have to face. I've reached rock bottom before and I've climbed out, I can do it again.

7
CHERRIES, WEBBED TOES & RAISIN FINGERS

2005

I can smell that smell again, the smell that comes just a day before someone gets sick. No one believes me but I can smell when someone is going to get sick and I'm never wrong. Today Tilly smells of the sick. I don't like her; she's very mean and looks at me funny whenever I talk. I don't really mind that she doesn't like me because she looks like a suede. She reminds me of the mash that my parents make that's not mash but they claim it is mash and when they don't put butter in it it's just plain nasty. It's made from mashed carrots and suede and that's what she looks like, with her ginger bob haircut and round face. The way she talks is like the weird suede mash too, she never says anything that's interesting, it's all about horses and that's boring. I don't mind horses, but I don't want to talk about them all day. I stare at Tilly as I smell the sick and I start to giggle quietly because I've compared her to a vegetable.

I always think of people as being like noun things, it helps me decide if I like people or not and put them into categories. Alex reminds me of a frog, and I don't much like frogs but he's nice, his eyelashes are different because they're so light and sometimes I wonder if they're even there at all. He's a nice friend and I think it would make him sad if I asked about his eyelashes, mum says I say mean things sometimes, but I don't mean to. I just speak aloud what I'm thinking in my head, and I find it confusing when other people don't do that, no one seems to say what they mean. Mum and dad have taught me to think my thoughts but not say them out loud.

Mrs Smith, my teacher in Year Three makes me think of a Koala because she has a Koala in the back of her car. I think it suits her because koalas are dark colours and she's a dark colour to me, grey or black maybe even dark purple. Mrs Smith scares me because she always used to tell me off for colouring in the wrong way and holding my pencil wrong. Everyone tells me I hold my pencil wrong but when I hold it their way it hurts my fingers, and they go all clicky after a while. My fingers bend more than all the other kids and they start to hurt after a while of doing things that make them bend too far. All the children think Mrs Smith is really mean, and I couldn't wait to be out of her class.

I like Nick the most, his hair is curly like mine, and he likes dinosaurs too. I think when I get older, I'd like him to be my boyfriend and for us to be in love like my mum and dad. Nick reminds me of ET because he's got a long neck and is taller than everyone else in our year. This year in the school play he's going to be Joseph and I'll be Mary and I think that means that he likes me too, I do really hope so. I can't wait to be Mary, but I don't like the thought of holding a baby. I don't like them; they make horrible noises that make me want to run away and I don't know what to do when they're around. I think I'd like to have a baby one day but maybe someone else can look after it when it cries and makes a mess. I hope I don't have a baby like me, I just cried all the time and wouldn't eat anything or sleep. Dad said I was always up and around, they had to hold me down to make me go to sleep every single night or I would be up and around my cot all night. Dad calls me a 'fidget-bum' always squirming around like a wriggly worm, never sitting still to watch TV and always needing them to keep me preoccupied. When I was first born, the nurses took me away from my mum in the hospital so she could sleep because all I did was cry and they didn't think it was very fair for mum. I don't think I've been a very good child for mum and dad, but I hope I have a good child.

I move away from Tilly so I can't smell the sick and settle on a seat next to Peter and Ben for lunch. Today it's my favourite: pasta with tomato sauce and cheese, I love all the ingredients, but I won't eat tomato ketchup at home, unless it's separate from everything else and I can have little bits at a time. I think about telling mum that I will eat pasta for breakfast but then I don't want to ruin pasta, because breakfast ruins everything, sometimes my whole day.

For dessert today, it's another of my favourites: fruit salad. I don't eat many of the puddings because they're not chocolate and lots of the time they have custard on them and that's just nasty, I don't like the smell and I hate it when other people are eating custard next to me because it makes me feel sick. I usually ask Mrs Howell if I can go outside to play early when people are eating custard. But today is fruit salad day and I can't wait to play our usual game of comparing our fruit. The fruit salad is a tinned one that is always the same, which is nice, mum asks why I won't eat this for breakfast, but it doesn't feel right at breakfast time because I have it for lunch and it's a school food not a home food. The cherries don't taste okay at home and they're the best bit, everyone who gets a cherry in their bowl is lucky and shows everyone else around them. I've got two today, that's never happened before, and I know Mrs Peters must like me best.

"I've got two cherries!" I boast, turning towards Peter and Ben, "look, look!"

"I'll give you three pears for it." Says Ben and Peter offers me two melons, but I refuse both of them, cherries can't be beaten and I save them until last in my bowl, like I do with everything I like best. Dad tells me that I should eat a little bit of everything on my plate at the same time, because then I get the flavours of everything all at once and that's okay but sometimes, I can't plan how much of my favourite thing I need to eat with each mouthful so that it's the last thing on my plate. If that happens, I get really upset and refuse to eat the rest of it and this makes everyone at the table mad. I feel angry when dad says these things anyway, he won't eat lots of things and likes things to be separate on his plate sometimes too, he won't eat mushy peas and brown sauce and mustard and gets really annoyed when my grandpa tells him he should eat mushy peas. I liked mushy peas with ketchup for a bit, but I don't like them anymore because they taste all squishy and grandpa says it confuses him how often I change my mind about food.

Mrs Howell enters the lunchroom and announces that there's music practice at playtime today instead of going outside and I don't like this, I like to go outside and play imaginary games on the AstroTurf. Mrs Allen, our music teacher keeps all mine and Linda's classes back after lunch to practice a silly song that I don't even like and it's just too noisy. Peter and Ben are playing the recorder at the right of me, and Sarah is playing her flute right in my left ear. Mrs Allen has given me a triangle to play, which I have to hold up in the air and hit with a metal stick in time with the beat. Everyone knows that the triangle is the easiest to play and the person who's the worst at music gets given it. This is tricky because I can't even clap my hands in time with everyone else and I can't control my hands properly after I've been clapping a while, so they do weird movements that I can't control, and my fingers start to feel fluffy.

I'm concentrating really hard on trying to tap the triangle at the right time and for a few minutes I get it but then I start to get confused by all the different noises in the room and there's no lyrics in the music to help me plan when to hit the triangle. It starts to get difficult to tap the triangle with the right force and I end up hardly hitting it and then hitting it to the floor. Mrs Allen sees this and tells me off for distracting everyone else and not taking our practice seriously. I want to tell her that I was actually trying really hard but before I get chance to explain she sends me out to play. I can't ever keep up with everyone else in music and I feel much better for getting away from the noise of it all. I drop my triangle in the music box and go to collect my outdoor shoes from the rack before venturing out into the spring air. My footsteps are light on the floor as I work to avoid the cracks in the stonework, happy to be outside in the quiet and cool. When I reach the playground, I sit on the boarder of the AstroTurf, outside the window where I can see all my classmates continuing their music lesson. There's no one here to play with because all of my friends are in inside and all of the younger students are playing silly games on the concrete area. I like the feeling of being by myself for a bit, I can finally relax and not think about how to act around everyone else, what I need to say and do and make sure I'm playing nicely and cooperatively.

From my perch I can see the back of everyone's heads through the window, I can hear them as they chat and smile while they play their instruments, why can't I enjoy music lessons? I can't talk to anyone or even smile while I'm playing an instrument because I have to think too hard.

When we have done school shows for our music, Mrs Allen tells me to look at the audience and smile and look like I'm enjoying myself, but I'm not enjoying myself, music is rubbish because I am rubbish at it and everyone knows it. Mrs Allen knows it, that's why she sent me out. Mum and dad know I'm rubbish at music and they tell me that that's okay because I can't be good at everything and I am good at lots of other things, but I don't like being rubbish at things, it makes me feel hot and I want to scream and run around because I get a tingly feeling in my legs and bum.

I'm good at writing and sports and being clever but I'm not good at music, drawing or fitting in and they're really important at school because I get left out if I'm not good at them. I feel left out at home sometimes, because mum and dad and Grandma Spain are really good at art, and I wonder why I'm not good at it too. No one in my family is good at writing like me. Mum says that it's more important that I'm good at sports because then we can all play games in our garden, like badminton and throwing and catching. My parents are very proud of me when I do well at sports, and I like the feeling I get when I win things. I'm very good at swimming and I beat everyone else in school, in my room I have tons of gold medals hung up from our swimming gala at school every year. Mrs Kent, our swimming teacher said I should go to Tiger Sharks to swim with other kids who are really good, but I don't like doing new things and I don't really like swimming. I like being in the water but I don't like the sounds in the swimming baths because it's so loud and echoes and makes my ears hurt, it's also really bright and hurts my eyes. The goggles are too tight on my head and when I get out the water my fingers look like raisins and I need to lick them lots, especially when I have to touch dry things like my towel and socks, it makes my mouth and nose feel nasty.

The kids at school laugh at me when I lick my fingers

lots and tell me I'm weird, adults have told me I need to stop licking my fingers because it's not hygienic, so I make myself sit on my fingers to stop me doing it but I can still feel them all weird and raisin-like under my bum and it makes me shuffle in my seat and get told off for not sitting still. Sometimes, I lick my fingers when I'm turning pages in a book or touching clothes that feel weird and I always get told off for this because it looks weird. Grandpa England does this lots too and he doesn't get told off. It's feels really, really uncomfortable if I can't lick my fingers, it makes me want to squeal like a pig, but I've done that before and people think I'm even weirder then.

* * *

At home that night, whilst she's chopping the vegetables for tea and I'm trying hard to do my homework that feels really silly because schoolwork should be kept at school, mum turns to me with a smile.

"Right, we've booked for you to go to Tiger Sharks. You start next weekend." She announces. My brain doesn't quite commute this, but I know I don't like what she's said. Tiger Sharks sounds scary; I'm scared of both sharks and tigers and both of them together don't sound appealing. Mum tells me that it is a club for children to compete who are really good at swimming and Mrs Kent has pushed for me to go because I could be a really good addition to their team; especially with how fast I am at breaststroke. Dad often says I'm so good at swimming because of my webbed toes, it must make me a bit faster than normal children and I wonder if I've evolved from a family of frogs and not humans, maybe that's why I feel so different.

"I don't want to go!" I protest but no one listens, I can't exactly explain why I don't want to do it but I know I just don't like swimming or competing at it because I get a sick feeling every time we go. Mum says I must just be nervous and that's normal.

*   *   *

A week later we drive all the way to a new swimming baths to do a training session with my new teammates. I feel out of place, sat in my swimming costume in the uncomfortable, plastic chair at the poolside. Everyone knows each other and they chat away, so I sit there and watch what's going on because that's what I do best. I realise I'm the odd one out, I'm so much smaller than everyone else there, they're all so much older, mum says that's because I'm much better at sport than everyone else my age and so I can do things with older kids. As a baby, everyone says I walked, climbed and rode a bike far quicker than what is normal, and no one could believe how small I was yet so active. I like this because it makes me feel good at something, but the older kids don't like this because I'm so much younger but much better than them. In my first turn in the pool, I finish my length quicker than all the other boys and girls and they all glare at me, after that no one will speak to me and I don't understand why. I don't want to go back to Tiger Sharks again, no one likes me but Mrs Kent.

Mrs Kent is a really good swimming teacher, sometimes I struggle to understand what adults want me to do but swimming is easy because Mrs Kent shows us what to do and doesn't give us lots of words and instructions. We had to practice our leg action out of the water and said we should do frog legs for breaststroke, and I liked that because my toes are like frogs' toes anyway. All the other children couldn't move their legs right and Mrs Kent told them all to look at me, which made me feel really important. Adults like me when I'm good at things but other children don't and that makes me feel worried, because it's horrible when other kids dislike me, it means they leave me out and say nasty things about me.

After the training has finished everyone piles into the changing rooms and it's so noisy I have to cover my ears with my towel. I rush to the safety of a bench in the corner of the room with my things and take my swimming cap off, exposing my sticky out ears and some of the other kids stare, point and laugh. I've got goggle marks round my eyes too where they've been too tight and I realise that maybe they're not laughing at my ears and eyes, maybe it's my raisin fingers. I lick them continuously while I get changed and the boy next to me asks me why I'm licking my fingers.

"Because they're like raisins, and they feel all funny" I say confused, wondering why he's asking such a silly question, surely everyone feels the same.

"Why are you even here?" Asks one of the older girls.

"Yeah, you're just a little baby." Her friend laughs. At that point, my mum enters the changing room and congratulates me on how well I did. I feel embarrassed, no one else has their mum here because they're all grown up and suddenly, I'm so aware of how babyish I am. All the other children smile sweetly at my mum and say "see you next week Harry" as if they all liked me and wanted me there. When we get in the car, I turn to my mum and tell her that the other kids were nasty to me and I don't want to go back next week.

"You're just being sensitive," she says, "you did amazing, everyone was very impressed with how well you swam and how tiny you are."

We lasted two more weeks of training and competing for Tiger Sharks before my pre-swim meltdowns got too much for mum and dad and they agreed I didn't have to go anymore. I have a meltdown every time I was made to go anywhere new, especially if I don't know people, it is scary and I can never quite explain how worrisome these things are for me.

*   *   *

Today is the day of the swimming gala, mum and dad and grandma and grandpa are coming to watch, as they have done every year since I was little. Every year I've enjoyed the joy of winning medals and seeing how happy that made my family, but today is different, I woke up with funny feelings in my tummy and I really didn't want to go to school. It's only four hours until the gala begins, and I've got so worried that I've started with a migraine, all the lights are especially loud today, and my head feels really distant from everything around me. Whenever there's a loud noise or a high pitch it rattles around my head and makes me feel extra sick. It's really hard to talk when my migraines start because my brain doesn't seem to work well with words, and I end up having to point and shrug whenever people try to make me speak. This morning I kept telling my teachers that I didn't feel good, and they wafted it off as pre-swimming gala nerves, which I kept saying it was not, they know that I get migraines lots and I have to take special medication for it. They didn't wait around for me to get better when I was sick on the playground, they called mum immediately then, they really didn't need to wait until I was sick to do that, they could have just listened to me.

When mum arrives to pick me up, I have my eyes closed and my hat halfway down my head, trying to cover my eyes and ears from all the loudness of school. My teachers put me outside in the sunlight to try and help but it didn't help because it was sunny and that made me feel even sicker, but I couldn't say anything because my words had gone. I push the hat into my eyes so that I can feel the pressure and see funky shapes and lights in the darkness, mum tells me to stop. Mum asks me if I can walk, and I give her my hand sign that means 'no' because shaking my head would only hurt more. She scoops me up in her arms and carries me to the car, which is comforting because I don't have to worry about where my legs, arms and head are, and I can just concentrate on not being sick.

The car ride is nasty, lots of backwards and forwards motions and I'm relieved when we finally make it into the house and straight up into my bedroom, prepared for me with blinds closed and cold temperature. The darkness envelopes me and I welcome it with open arms, falling into a deep, undisturbed unconsciousness even before mum has left the room.

A few hours later, I wake to the feeling of cold hand shaking me softly and a cold towel is pressed to my forehead. My eyes flicker open, taking in the room, that seems a little lighter than before and slowly I meet mum's eyes.

"Are you ready to get up sweetheart? It's time for the swimming gala soon and I'd really like you to eat something before we go." Mum speaks in hushed tones, knowing normal voices are too loud for my migraine state. I really don't want to go to the swimming gala, where I know there's going to be noise and my sick feelings are going to come back again. I hatch a plan in my mind to make mum happy by getting up and having a bite to eat before returning to bed. I put on my favourite, purple hat, covering the tops of my eyelids, keeping my head down and away from the lights above. My purple hat is wooly, and it has my name 'Harry' knitted into it at the front. At the kitchen table, mum slides a plate towards me with a few slices of French bread with butter and half a chopped-up apple, she knows not to push it too far when I've had a migraine because I'll only throw it up again. I nibble the edges of the food, taking small and slow mouthfuls that don't shock my stomach, mum smiles, the plan is working.

"Come on then, go and put on your swim stuff." Mum smiles warmly, taking away the finished plate. I shake my head slowly and hide my face away; she isn't going to like this.

"I don't think I can go mum; I feel too poorly." It's a lie, we both know that I've recovered, or I wouldn't have got up and eaten some food. She smells the lie immediately.

"Come on Harry, dad will be there soon, and he was so excited to see you swim this afternoon." My mind flashes back to the morning's events where he kissed the top of my head before leaving for work and flashed me a wide grin. "I'm so proud of you, my little piranha." He had said, before picking up his briefcase, lunchbox and car keys, looking back to smile at me before he shut the front door. I love making dad proud and I know I can't let him down; I must go to the swimming gala. Reluctantly, I leave the room and find my swimming outfit in the kit bag mum had sent me to school with this morning. As I slide the swimming costume over my body, it feels strange, my body feels too exposed, and I just want to stay hidden under my 'Harry' hat and oversized jumper. It feels more difficult to hide my true self when I'm wearing just a swimming costume, there's nothing to distract from my curled toes, and nails dug into palms and licked fingers.

I see my unmade bed out of the corner of my eye and think about how wonderful it will be to crawl back in and shut out the world, pulling the covers over my tired eyes and pretending I'm somewhere else. Instead of succumbing to my desires, I turn to look in the mirror next to me and practice my smile that I must give when I win my medal and all my family and friends congratulate me. The smile looks all wrong, like it belongs on someone else because my feelings inside just don't match. I place my fingers inside my mouth and stretch the corners into a big grin, holding it in place for as long as I can bear the pain. I don't feel pain in the same way when I've experienced a migraine, everything feels duller afterwards and so I can stretch my grin longer today. I must look pleased, I must look grateful, and I must look happy.

Mum drives us to the gala, my head in buried

underneath my swim towel; I'm trying so hard to block out the outside world so that I can be on my best behaviour when we get to the pool. Mum doesn't understand this, and she tells me to take the towel from my head and speak to her. My words can't come out now, I silently beg that she doesn't push me into speech because that will only make things worse later when I get tired and ratty, and I'm mean to her. I wish she could just understand that me being quiet is me saving all my words and energy for the people she's taught me to be polite and talkative with. I continue to wrap the towel around my head, leaning on the window, pretending to be asleep.

The next hour is a blur of noise and movement that I can't keep up with and all of a sudden, I find myself, for the first time since we left the car, completely aware of my surroundings and body as I stand at the side of the pool. I curl my toes over the side of the pool edge, my 'monkey feet' I call them when they grip onto anything. I gaze into the clear water below, feeling the nerves emanate from the children beside me. We stand together, only inches apart at the starting line ready for the whistle to blow, anxious anticipation is abundant in the air.

Time seems to stand still, I'm not sure how I got to the side of the pool, but I feel grounded with my feet are curled over the edge, embracing the sensation of the cold water nibbling at my toes. The whistle blows to signal we must assume our starting positions, a shrill and deafening sound that makes me ears feel like they're bleeding, diving into the water is the only option I have to escape the noise that comes rushing in. Simultaneously, all my senses become hyper-aware, the lapping of the pool the chatter of spectators, my goggles being too tight on my head and eyes. I dig my nails into my palms and tighten the grasp of my toes on the edge of the pool. Everyone's eyes are on me, and I really don't like it, I want to be back in my bedroom with the covers up high and the lights off. I've tried to tell everyone today that I don't want to be here, and it was too much for me but no one listened; no one ever seems to listen to what I want. I'm always told that I should make an effort to do things that other people want me to do but no one ever seems to listen to what I want to do. I don't want to be here at the edge of this pool, surrounded by people in discomfort and panic, but they wouldn't know about the panic because I have to hide it all inside and be polite to everyone.

I try so, so hard to be a good girl and go to the swimming galas and birthday parties and school events and be polite to everyone, make sure I speak and play fairly, and like everyone else and smile. I'm so tired whenever we do those things, or when I have to be good all day at school that I run out of words and good behaviour for being at home and I'm really nasty to mum. I really try very hard to be a good girl when I get home but there are too many tasks and words and expectations that I can't do it all day and then all evening, it's too much. I want to make everyone proud, all my family have come to watch me win my race and I will win my race but everything in me wants to run away and hide in the changing rooms or even further away, maybe alone in the woods somewhere with Scruffy, where no one will be around to expect things from me. I want to run out the doors, down the road and into the trees where no one can find me, for a really long time but I can't. My feet are glued to the tiles, my eyes fixed in position at the end of the pool lane, my body doesn't feel like my own, it's all numb and disconnected. I suddenly wonder if Peter in the next lane ever feels like this, does he question if his body belongs to him? Does he want to run away too? Does he feel frightened of what he will behave like when he gets home? Is he scared that one day his emotions and his reactions will just get too much for his parents and they won't want him anymore? I hope he doesn't wonder all those things and I know deep down that he doesn't, no one else around me does, but still, it would be nice not to be the only one.

The water below my feet gnashes at the corners of its container in an attempt to escape. Just like me, caged, entrapped, bounded. I think of the calm water when there's been no one in it, it's peaceful and slow moving, content in its boundaries. But then someone jumps in and invades its space, thrashing about and unsettling the equilibrium, if only the water could be left alone. I think of myself, happy in my bedroom, undisturbed reading books, writing stories and moving my toys into categories of colour and preference. It's only when people disturb my safe space that things go wrong, when I'm given instructions, given food I can't stomach, taken to places I feel uncomfortable and unable to be myself, forced into talking. I'm alike to the water below me; internally I thrash around trying to break out of my restrictions and obligations, screaming and crying on the inside, but looking like a calm body of water on the exterior. I look again at Peter, he smiles at me excitedly, his expression doesn't change in response to my expression, and can he not see what's going on inside me? I realise I've mirrored his smile without even being aware.

What must the other children see when they look at me? A smatter of freckles, curly, auburn hair? A tomboy who doesn't fit in with the outfits the other girls wear? Someone different from themselves, trapped, pressured? I know for sure they don't see me as I am, no one does, only my teddies see me as I am, safe to unmask in the comfort of my bedroom or the bushes in our garden. Only in these sacred places can I unveil the essence of who Harry is. But not here, not in the confines of the swimming gala, with everyone's eyes on me. I know now what the audience of family members see: a good girl who doesn't step outside the lines, is shy but polite, she writes stunning stories and is a teacher's pet, she's quirky and her humour replicates that of her dad. I wish I could be that girl but it's not the truth.

The whistle blows and my body snaps into action,

plummeting into the water below me, hitting me with an initial wave of shock, it feels like a long time before my arms and legs start to paddle. Being underneath the water feels refreshing, the sounds are dulled and there's a wall between me and everyone else in the room, I can be me under the water. I begin to cry underneath my goggles, knowing that no one will ever know of my sadness. The relief of the water is brief as I pull up to the surface for air, seeing Peter and Ben yards behind me, coming back into awareness of the echoes along the poolside and the brightness of the lights. I shut my eyes, squishing the water out of them and into the bottom of the goggles.

I dream of being elsewhere and disconnect from the overwhelming noises, sights and smells around me. I transport myself into a part of my body where no one will find me, the back of my mind – dissociation, I start to re-run my favourite film – Shrek – scene by scene in my mind, knowing every single word and sequence. I feel safe in the knowledge that my brain isn't aware enough to recall the distressing events of the rest of the day. I finish all the races first, in autopilot. Though I don't recall it, I receive my gold medals just like every other year and I'm cooed over by all the parents, "Wow she's such a talented child," they say to mum and dad, "you must be so proud". My parents smile and nod, but they give nothing away of what it's really like to be my family. If only they knew, the little girl who seems so put together on the outside could be so unbelievably damaged on the inside.

8
THE COLOUR CO-ORDINATED CADDY

Warning: Discussion of self-harm and suicidal ideation throughout.

May 2022

It's been over six years since my last external, golf competition and the nerves are beginning to cripple me as I draw closer to my destination on Google maps. Until this year, I hadn't felt ready mentally to compete again both because of anxiety and organisational skills. It's apparent now, after my diagnosis, why I could never quite get around to filling in the forms, researching the competition dates, organising partners to play with. It seemed that as soon as I moved out of my family home and became less dependent on them, I lost all interest in golf but that really wasn't the case, although no one understood me no matter how hard I tried to explain it. I couldn't even explain it to myself; I just put it down to feeling depressed or being shattered.

In reality, I loved those competitions, they always made me feel very anxious, but they were some of my favourite times with my parents. We would travel all across the country, making a mini holiday out of the event, staying in idyllic countryside cottages and sometimes near the sea. Every morning of the competition, I would get up with a feeling of extreme anxiety, worrying immediately that I was late for my tee time or that I wouldn't have packed the right equipment. That anxiety lessened once I knew I had my parents next door to organise and support me the whole day, especially with my dad caddying for me. Dad has always had a way of understanding me without words, he can look at me during a golf round and know when I need time to be silent, when I need to talk incessantly and when I need a cooling off period. Mum has not always been so aware, she's always filled every silence and tried to help even when help is clearly not wanted, I love my mum to bits but definitely not as a caddy!

Hiding my anxiety in sport has always been easy for me, because I mastered masking from such a young age, I knew how to intimidate an opponent, how to walk and talk with confidence. I turned up to the course each morning exuding no signs of worry, shutting everyone out with my headphones and putting myself in the zone. I almost convinced myself I was as confident as I appeared but the problem with this was, it was all a mask and at the end of the day I would be physically *and* mentally exhausted. Still, I loved it.

I remind myself of the incident at my competition and remind myself: *today will not be like that*. I sit at the traffic lights flapping my hands frantically, a new stim I tried out that seems to work at lowering my anxiety. I don't feel comfortable enough to stim in front of other people yet so I need to get it all out before I get to the golf club and I'm surrounded by other people, the thought momentarily disables my bodily functions and I find myself stuck at a green light. A beep behind me snaps me back into my body and I continue the drive.

I'm later than I anticipated, as always, but this time I planned to get to the club ridiculously early so that I wouldn't be so stressed out. I've spent the whole drive calculating exactly how much time I will have to eat my breakfast, check in, practice, set up my equipment and get to the first tee, over and over again my head. By the time I reach the club, I'm exhausted. The car park is almost empty, and I start to panic that I have the wrong date, as I have many times before, but turning the corner, I see the familiar Yorkshire Golf green jumpers and feel my shoulders relax instantly. *Okay, first thing go check in* I prompt myself, but my body doesn't move, fixed due to the next transition meaning social time and a flurry of different organisational and cognition-heavy activities. I allow my body to catch up with my brain, this is something that happens regularly; I learnt it has a name: autistic inertia. I must ride it out, like I do most days where I come home from work and sit in the car on the drive each evening for around twenty minutes. It's almost like having to reboot the brain after the events of the day so that I can move into the next stage of the day.

Finally, my body feels ready for the next step, and I drag my heavy-feeling limbs out of the car and start to unpack my equipment, going to check in and speak feels too much at present. I avoid eye contact with the surrounding women, thankfully none of which I know, I'm not ready to meet their gaze or exchange pleasantries just yet. I can see how this could be seen as rude and why so many times in the past I've been viewed as unapproachable, which has always saddened me, as I'm a friendly person, I just need to interact in my own time. Packing up my food and checking I have all the things I need I quickly realise that my headphones are missing, and a feeling of uncertainty starts to build up in my body. My headphones are a safety blanket, especially when I go somewhere new or loud, they block out the rest of the world and consume me in what makes me happiest: music. How could I have been so disorganised? They are the first things I should always pack because the world without them is insufferable! *It's okay, I'll just keep my distance from people,* I tell myself and continue to organise my kit. I become acutely aware that dad isn't going to be here for another half hour and that doesn't help the situation, if he were here earlier then maybe I could cope, he could help me block it all out.

Hesitantly, I tear myself away from checking for the seventh time I have everything I need and walk towards the clubhouse in search of the registration desk. *Just get the worst part over with,* I think as the anxiety mounts once again. What if I can't find the desk? What if no one is there? What if they've changed my tee time to be earlier? There are so many possibilities, it all feels overwhelming and takes me three attempts to walk through the threshold of the registration office.

"Hello." I introduce myself loudly, a large, fake smile plastered across my face, fight or flight activated, my body stiff and my mask firmly in place. "Harry Richardson." I'm completely unaware of anyone in the room, focused only on the woman behind the desk, I quite possibly have interrupted a conversation but I'm impulsive when I'm stressed.

"Here you go." The lady stops sifting through the scorecards and hands me mine, 09:57 written next to my name, *thank God, no time change.* She begins to speak about something else, but I've checked out, only to zone back into her words at the end of what she's saying. She's gestured to a piece of paper, so I pick up what she's pointing to.

"Can I take this?" I ask, clutching the sheet in front of me with pin positions.

"No, like I said, just take a picture of this." Obviously, following her gesture wasn't enough; I needed to listen to her words too. This happens often, I don't always follow what people say and so I have to follow all of their movements, facial expressions and cues in my environment to tell me what they've just said or are asking me to do, it's all very draining. Now I'm confused, the sign outside the clubhouse read **no phones past this point**, I study her face, looking for any more clues about what to do, should I listen to the sign or this woman who isn't giving anything away with her face. I decide to trust her words and snap a picture of the pin positions, pin for the toilet on the course and the phone number for the course referee.

"Thank you!" I grin even wider, which seems to make them believe this interaction is comfortable for me. They wish me good luck on my round and other typical pre-match phrases; I tune out again needing to escape the room and retreat into solitude. Gathering some golf balls for the range, I march off to the practice ground, already anxious that I'm not going to squeeze in all of the practice I want to before the round, I didn't allow time for autistic inertia and hesitance to enter the clubhouse. I see a group of women hitting balls as I approach the range and race past them, settling on the bay furthest away so that I don't get myself involved in idle chit-chat. They all seem to know each other and discuss the rules of the competition, a document we were sent in an email a few weeks ago, just like every other document, I wasn't able to read. All the information staring back at me on the screen was too much to digest, no visual information and all the words I tried to read didn't make sense, so I gave up. I close my ears to the conversation and put up my invisible wall to block them out. As my tee time draws closer, I start to worry about the time but my time to stim has ended, I don't want to do it in public just yet.

From the corner of my eye, I catch a glimpse of a man

approaching and the anxiety starts to subside as I recognise my dad, my safety blanket, with his hands in his pockets, equally as anti-social as me towards the other women on the range. I smile as he draws closer and realise he's also wearing blue.

"I see you got the memo about team colours then?" I laugh.

"Huh?" He looks at me blankly until I gesture to the blue top I'm wearing and his own jumper a few shades lighter. Conversation with dad is peaceful; we don't have to greet each other with politeness, instead just saying whatever we want to rather than going through all the social niceties of conversation initiation. I'm aware that people find me bizarre when I often answer the phone to Jack with 'what's up?' rather than saying hello and asking about his day. We don't need to cover the basics of conversation, what's the point? If he wants me to know about his day he will tell me, I want the phone call to be short and to the point because I hate the phone anyway. Even dad finds it odd sometimes the way I communicate with Jack, it's so brief and emotionless over the phone. Jack has come to expect and accept this.

After some time on the chipping green, dad prompts me that it's nearly the tee time and I need to get to the putting green first. I'm thankful for his help; I would have completely run out of time if he weren't there.

"How do you feel about carrying my bag for thirty-six holes?" I tease dad as I pick up my golf bag, throwing it over my shoulders.

"Ahhh." He groans, "I got a bad back from DIY yesterday." Dad always has his hands busy with some sort of project, whether that's building something for the house, sketching some building designs or taking things apart only to put them together again and understand how they work. Lego is one of his favourite activites and it's something he certainly passed on to me and my brother, Alex as we grew up. We approach my car and I unload the trolley and battery, having joked about dad carrying the bag, there's no way I'd do that to him at his age.

"Oh you've brought your trolley!" He laughs, "Thanks for having me on."

"As if I'd make you carry my bag for thirty-six holes!" Sometimes, people don't get my jokes; they don't understand why it's funny when I wind them up with comments that aren't true. I don't know why I like doing that so much, I guess I like to see people's reactions to absurd things before I tell them I'm joking. It annoys Jack regularly and he frequently tells me he doesn't get my humour. Dad is used to it after twenty-six years and allows me my moment of enjoyment.

As we approach the tee my mask is pulled on tighter than ever, my smile seems one-hundred percent genuine but really, I just want to turn away from everyone and everything. I know the girl next to me is going to be my playing partner, but I can't work myself up to make eye contact or say hello just yet, I'm only focused on the fact that I know the starter on the tee and I'm going to have to script some conversation with her before I get to the tee. Janice is a member at my golf club and I've known her for several years, including working with her daughter for some time behind the bar at the club. That's when I gather my plan for conversation, I will ask her about her daughter and I'm sure we won't get stuck.

"Hi Janice!" I smile broadly at her as I walk towards the first tee. "Long time no see." I hate the phrase but it's something I hear everyone say and everyone seems to respond well to it. Often, I use sentences without even thinking it through, the ones I use regularly come out great just like this and others I'm less familiar with come out in the wrong order and I embarrass myself. *Stick to what you know,* I tell myself before walking into a conversation.

"Harry, hello, how are you?" Her eyes widen with her smile as she sees me and starts to approach me for a hug. I knew this would happen, it always does, all the ladies at the club always hug me and sometimes kiss me on the cheek and it's honestly the worst. I can never read a person's body language to know if they're going to give me a hug or kiss me because I'm too consumed with the worry about how awful it's going to feel when they touch me. Janice envelopes me in a hug, and goes to kiss my cheek but I've leant too far in and instead she's got my ear, it's all a bit of a mess and something that happens regularly, I hate it. I've been trying to tell people close to me to stop hugging me and touching me unexpectedly and that's easy but telling people I don't know not to touch me is just awkward and so I continue to do what I've always done: hide the discomfort, grin and bear it.

"I'm great thanks." *I'm horrible, this is horrible, I don't want to be touched and now my whole body feels wrong and squirmy,* I think but don't verbalise. "How's Holly doing?" She tells me all about her daughter travelling and the work she's doing, and it feels great just to listen and know that I've hit the nail on the head with my choice of conversation topic. It's always great when I find something that allows the other person to do a monologue and I can just sit back and relax, not needing to give anything to further the conversation. Janice then introduces me to my playing partner; we exchange smiles and a handshake, which feels okay because it's firm and quick. She quickly passes me her scorecard and identifies her golf ball; as usual I'm slow to the mark and jostle around in my bag for the scorecard and a new ball. I can never be as organised as everyone else at golf and I understand now that's all to do with executive functioning difficulties. I was always the person to turn up to the tee late, without the right equipment, the wrong clothes to match the weather and no awareness of the rules and social expectations. It's been a source of great embarrassment over the years. The worst has been when I've given my score to people at the end of my round, I can't hold in information related to how many shots I've had, how many my opponent has had, who has won the hole and how many I am ahead. I've been laughed at and told I'm dizzy time and time again because I can never quite get it right as hard as I try.

Golf has always suited me, the slow pace of it allows me thinking time and regulation between shots, unlike tennis, which always made me rage if I started playing badly. My focus is unbreakable; helicopters have flown over me whilst I'm taking a shot without any recognition. I completely concentrate on my own game, being in competition with myself and no one else. Many people have commented that I don't seem phased or put under pressure by my opponent during match play but that's just because in my mind I'm not competing with them, I actually have no idea how many shots they've had so why would I feel pressure?

The only thing that would make golf better for me is if there wasn't so much expectation for me to communicate. I'm happiest when I'm walking around the course by myself or with Meeno, with my headphones in and in complete silence. I'm focused on my game, singing songs in my head and preparing myself for the next shot. My family always push me to play with other people, get someone to mark me a card and socialise but I rarely enjoy that side of golf. Playing golf with other people means having to snap out of my focused state, make small talk I'm not very good at and keep up with fragmented conversations between taking turns to hit the ball. Instead of putting my mental energy into my game, it's distracted by thoughts of what to ask someone about themselves next, what we were talking about before our conversation broke off and worrying about whether I'm being chatty enough or too chatty. It's honestly exhausting.

Finally, Janice announces my name and gestures for me to start play. I stand on the golf tee, reminding myself that this is the first competition since the incident. It's been six years now and I still haven't been able to shift the memory out of my focus. I need to concentrate on the game in front of me now, but the feelings come rushing back and I'm right back there.

September 2017

I sit in the back of my parent's car, silent. Not just silent with words but vacant, every corner of my body is without feeling. Now and again panic will break the surface and I'll cry desperate tears, wanting to beg them to stop the car and turn back around. I want to go home but letting people down feels worse than carrying on, so I suppress the panicked pleas and continue to stare straight ahead.

Last night, I woke at midnight in nightmares. In my dreams I was back at university, my head barely above the water, drowning. I couldn't breathe. I woke breathless, without the right rhythm in my breath, all the air going out but nothing going in. I sob, unable to gather my thoughts between the gulps for air. The trauma of university is haunting the entire room and I can't escape it, the memories are overpowering, as if they're happening over again.

Suddenly, my skin starts to feel wrong all over my body and I scratch it, trying to tear it off from my bones. I want to get out of my body because it just feels completely wrong in every way and at every edge, from my fingertips to my toes. But I can't escape, I'm trapped in the sensory torture, and I just can't breathe. The feeling has to stop. I do the only thing I can to alleviate the distress, scrapping my nails across my skin until it breaks. That's no good, it's not enough. Reaching into my bedside drawer my fingers find my hidden worst enemy and drag it across my skin, my arms my hips and my legs. I'm not thinking of consequences or what has happened in the past, I just need to escape this feeling.

It's the worst injury I've ever had, and I scream, panicking. Almost immediately my parents burst into the room, concern covering their faces. My mum looks from me to my leg and orders my dad to get some things from the bathroom. The panic reduces instantaneously, my parents are here, it's going to be okay. The feelings of needing to be out of my skin don't dissipate, but their presence reassurances me I'm not alone in the torment anymore. Mum holds me tightly as dad presses tissues to my skin, trying light pressure to avoid pain, but the pain hardly registers, the rest of my body is on fire, it's nothing in comparison.

"Why didn't you come and wake us up?" Mum says, tears continuing to seep from her eyes.

"I don't know." I mutter without inflection, unable to connect with feeling, a glass wall between me and everything else. 'I'm supposed to stop this from happening' my dad had said almost ten years ago, when he first learnt of my self-harm. He pressed his body to mine in the longest hug we'd ever had, it had so much meaning and intensity and I felt him cry, the first time I'd ever seen my dad cry. The sudden emotion overwhelmed me, and I had promised not to do this again because I couldn't bear the thought of making my dad cry. But here we are, ten years later in the same situation, this time dad not crying, numb to the situation over the years.

Mum continues to hold me as I scream and cry and try to hit myself all over my body, I need to escape this situation, but I can't and nothing my parents do can make it any better. I just need to world to stop so I can get off and just be. Be alone, feel calmness and not want to scrape off my skin. I feel as though I'm outside of my body, I no longer recognise my movements and I can't control them. The screams that come out of me don't feel like my own and I don't recall allowing my body to make them. This is dissociation, my body is no longer mine and I see myself from a different position than the one I'm sat in. This is exactly how I felt late at night in my university bedroom, trapped but without anyone to call for help. I feared being alone because that meant there was no one there to stop this unpredictability and chaos. So instead, each night I went out with people to the early hours of the morning because it was easier than being alone. I hid the pain and discomfort with alcohol until I couldn't hide anymore. I never wanted to stop living, I just wanted the pain to end because I couldn't bear to continue living in a body that felt uncomfortable and a mind that wouldn't wind down or stop reliving my worst memories. I just wanted the world to stop for a while so I could catch up, so I could have a break. I never wanted it all to end, but that's where I ended up.

How did I end up here? I think as I lay awake for the next hour, mum holding me from the space in the bed next to me.

And now, I'm headed to a golf competition with bandages around my left arm and my leg held together with plasters bigger than my hand. Mum had begged me to go to the hospital, but nothing could be worse than having a meltdown and then going to a place that causes meltdowns. I decided a huge scar was the better option. As we pull into the drive to the golf club, panic sets in and it feels difficult to breathe. Suddenly, I don't think I can do this. I pull at my clothes, panicking that people will ask me about the bandages, someone will see the plasters underneath my skort. They'll all know, they'll all judge what they don't understand. It's a bright summer's day and there's no way I could wear trousers or a jumper. For the first time in my life, I can't hide my emotions, I can't hide my fragile state of mind. I can't hide the physical evidence, but I also can't hide behind my mask this time. I can't put a smile on today and pretend nothing has happened. I can't pretend I'm a happy-go-lucky, positive energy, when less than 3 months ago I tried to end my life. The meltdown last night has made me so exhausted that there is no façade today, no matter how much I want there to be. It's scary to admit to myself for the first time, people will see what is underneath the smile, the pretense, the dishonesty; they'll see the real, hard facts. Likely, they won't like what they see.

Mum gets out of the car and approaches the team captain, a lady that is too bubbly and lively for me today and explains that I'm not feeling very well, I've hurt my wrist, but I still really want to play for the team. She explains that my dad is going to caddy for me the whole round because I'm so anxious and I need the support. I know that is what she is saying because that's what we planned for her to say. I watch the facial expressions of the captain set in, she's concerned, she knows there's more to the story. Her smile faded very quickly, and she looks uncomfortable, obviously unsure what to say. I really want to tell dad to go over there and tell her I'm not playing, to just drive me home without saying anything to anyone else but the words don't come out of my mouth. I zone out of the conversation going on outside and realise dad has been talking to me, but I wasn't processing it, I catch the end of what he's saying.

"Just remember, if you need to stop playing, just let me know and we can leave. Just at least give it a try, I'm sure you'll feel better when you get started." Sometimes, I wonder how they believe the things they say, nothing is going to make me feel better in this moment, other than escaping and being far away from this whole situation. Do they truly believe the things they say?

I ignore dad and rest my forehead on the window. From this position, I can see the girls on my team gathered around, practicing, chatting and laughing with each other. Sure, I get on with them and I like them and I'm sure they like me, but I've never felt like part of a real team. I turn up, I play and then I don't know what to say to them when they structure falls down, what do we talk about when what we came here to do has finished? I've never felt able to fit in here and today is definitely not going to be the day that changes.

"Come on, you better get your bag ready and get

practicing." Dad gets out of the car and heads to the boot to gather my things. I briefly wonder what my parents think of having a daughter that has cut her skin to pieces and 3 months ago didn't want to be part of this world. What must that feel like for them? I remember in my worst days feeling that they wouldn't mind so much if I wasn't here. All the times I stressed them out and made mum cry and they sat around the kitchen table trying to work out how to fix me and make things better, when they should have just been enjoying their evening. No parent wishes for a child like this, why would they?

I drag my heavy feet out of the car as dad opens the door, everything feels heavy and everything hurts, I'm not sure how I'm supposed to play golf. Immediately, I avoid everyone's gaze and busy myself with sorting out my equipment. Tears prick in my eyes and quickly start to roll down my face as I realise that I'm here and I'm actually going to have to play a game of golf after the events of last night. Until now, it's been incomprehensible. The lady captain obviously has spread the news of me being unwell because people avoid me as much as possible and try to give me some space as I pass. I realise everyone is saying hello to me but I can't summon the words I need to respond, at every corner dad speaks for me. I'm switched off to the rest of the world, nothing they say is processing and all I can think about is the bandages that everyone's eyes are drawn to. *What are they all thinking?*

Somehow, I manage to play golf. Somewhere along the way, I crouch down, having a moment of mini panic, which no one but dad seems to notice. I'm not here, I'm in a different world, and this doesn't feel like reality. I carry on going through the motions whilst in the midst of a panic attack. I hit a shot onto the green next to the pin, even though I can't breathe, and everyone claps. *Are they not aware?* How could they be aware? This girl just hit a professional-standard golf shot for the fourth hole in a row, why would anyone ever believe she's feeling disconnected from her whole body and can't breathe through the panic?

On the sixteenth hole, a buggy drives up the fairway, alerting our match and everyone watching that the team has won, so this game can cease. The relief is overwhelming, so overwhelming that I rush to shake the hand of my opponent and bolt off the course, crumpling into the arms of both of my parents. No one has any idea of the turmoil I'm in and I don't understand how. My parents are literally carrying me to the car, my plaster hasn't managed to conceal my wound, which is now bleeding down my leg and I'm crying. They don't realise so much that just as I think I'm safe from the crowds, they call me over for a team photo. I throw on a jumper and tug the sleeves down over my hands, my knees trembling. Team members throw their arms around me and squeeze in for a photo and I can hardly believe my legs are holding me up, this is hell and I need to *go*. As soon as photos are over, my parents quickly bundle me into the car, giving me a hoody to hide in and mum rushes to make our excuses to the team that I feel so ill we need to go home right away, instead of celebrating with everyone else. I wonder what everyone else's lives are like, whilst they smile and enjoy the day and pause to consider that none of them experience things like this. None of them feel this vulnerable, damaged, broken. None of them experience these meltdowns that last for days. None of them really know what it is like to be me, because I'm not normal, I'm not like them. I never have been.

I've never felt so exposed, so vulnerable. Even though I showed it for the very first time, no one even seemed to notice. I realised then that no one really pays attention to me, they never really have. Everyone sees what they want to see, and no one wants to see the pain I'm in.

September 2023

The phone connects to my dad as I finish writing the chapter. I need to know how he feels about what I'm about to share with the world, because I'm not too sure that I should. Self-harm and suicidal ideation are hard to talk about and it's a topic that makes people uncomfortable. It's something that I've always been told to conceal because it leaves you vulnerable and open to rejection. The stigma around mental health is still so rife, regardless of whether it's now discussed in the media. And a woman, at the age of twenty-two having an autistic meltdown of this propensity is not something that people talk about, it's kept under wraps. It's considered shameful when it shouldn't be.

"Hey dad, I've decided to re-write a chapter of my book, the one about you being a caddy and doing my first golf competition since the incident, I assume you know which incident I mean?" He agrees, "I just want to know your thoughts about whether I should write about that day. It's quite a difficult topic to read and might be a lot for people."

"Harry, I think that's the intention for what you are writing. You need people to listen to and hear your experience as it is. That's the power of what you're writing. It's not meant to be pretty."

"Okay, that's all I need to hear to confirm my decision." I smile, thankful that he gets my intentions. "I know it'll be hard for you to read, well actually, would it? You were there so you know what happened."

"Of course, it will be a difficult read. I was there, sure, but I didn't know what was going on in your head and what you were experiencing. That will be hard to read." And it strikes me that really, unless I tell people exactly what the experience is like of having an autistic meltdown, no one will ever understand, even when they have seen it with their own eyes. I have to finish the story I'm writing, and I have to include the things I never dreamt I'd write about.

9
MORRISON'S, MELTDOWNS & BACON

2004

It's a rainy Thursday; I stare out of the car window on the way to Morrison's for our weekly food shop, the worst part of my week. As we near the shop, mum starts to talk to me about tennis, she tells me I'm going to a new tennis center to do some extra training with my favourite coach, Tony. I love having lessons with Tony, he's really kind and helps me to understand things simply when they are a bit too difficult to understand. I love tennis too, I started playing tennis at four and I'm really good at it, I play almost every day and I don't have many friends at tennis but it's okay because I just love running around and hitting the ball. It's one of my favourite things to do, along with playing with Alex, my dog Basil and being with mum and dad. I play at the local tennis club, just down the road from my house and I go so often that I could close my eyes on the drive there and know exactly where I am, knowing every bend in the road. Sometimes, I close my eyes and just to test myself and I'm right almost every time.

I don't like to talk on my way to the tennis club because I like to plan what I'm going to say to people and which of my favourite characters I'm going to be like today. When mum drives me to the club she talks to me all the way there, it annoys me because I don't have the energy to chat, and I need to focus. The tennis club can be a difficult place to be sometimes because I have to walk through a cafe first, which has lots of people in who are all chatting and usually they want to say 'hello Harry' even when I try to avoid their eyes. People say that means I can seem rude but it's because I can't concentrate on what people are saying to me when there's lots of other people talking. I also never know what people want me to say to them because they ask random questions that don't have an exact answer, like 'how's school?' I don't know how much they want to me to tell them or what they want to exactly know and most of the time I don't think they really care so I don't know why they ask; they don't even know where I go to school.

The outdoor courts are nice in the summer because it's never too noisy or busy and I've got space to breathe. The indoor courts echo, and I can hear the screech of trainers on tarmac, which hurts my ears and makes me tense up. I can listen to the tennis coaches Dave and John, when we're in the outdoors but their words get muddled with the background noises indoors and I have to copy what everyone else is doing so that I don't annoy them by getting things wrong. Sometimes, I'm not supposed to be doing what everyone else is doing and so they get annoyed at me anyway. Dave and John always seem really confused that I'm so clever at school and they often tell me I'm not listening properly to their instructions because if I can get good marks at school then I should be able to answer their questions and follow their instructions. But the things they say sometimes aren't clear and I feel really lost, most lessons I panic because I can hear their words but there's too many of them and I know I won't be able to hold any of them in my head. It feels like the words are whizzing past my ears and I hear them, but I can't catch them and keep them in my ears and the more I try the worse it gets until I forget everything that they've said. I get so worried because I know they're going to be cross with me but the more I worry the harder it gets.

Tony isn't like that; he explains things one thing at a time and shows me actions with instructions so that I don't have to just listen. I really want to do some more lessons with Tony, but he's moved tennis clubs now and I don't want to go somewhere new. As hard as my tennis club is and how confusing the adults are, I don't like it when I have to go somewhere new, I'd rather stay where I'm comfortable.

Mum tells me all about the new club and what it will be like but all I can think about is how much I hate food shopping. It takes too long, and mum always has to look at every single different item to check which is best before putting it in the trolley. There's too much noise, too many smells and too many people. I have to push the trolley and people get in my way and mum tries to pull the trolley, which annoys me more because I like to go at my own pace and never be pulled, I don't like the feeling. I'm upset that I'm having to go to the shop, and I'm upset that she's making me go to a new tennis club, one is enough but the two together gives a wave of insurmountable emotion. I start to cry uncontrollably as we drive along and scream at her that I don't want to go somewhere new, especially when all the kids are older than me and they all know each other. I want to tell her that I find it hard to get on with the kids I do know at my normal tennis club and how hard it is for me to meet new people because no one ever likes me, and I'm always laughed at and left out but I don't know how to say it when I'm so upset.

"You need to stop being ridiculous, Harry. If you don't

like it when you go, you don't have to go again." But I know that's not what happens, they always make me try and go again and then again when I'm made to try something new. No one ever seems to listen to how much I don't want to do things. It's not that I don't want to it's that I can't, it all feels way too much. I'm screaming and crying and unable to talk between sobs and I can't think of anything worse right now than meeting new people. Mum won't let me stay in the car and I enter the shop with a blotchy face and puffy eyes, everyone stares, and it all feels too much. The lights are bright, there's too much noise and too many people, all staring at me. I *hate* people staring at me. I hate it! I hate it! I hate it! I want everyone to go away, I want to scream and hit everyone that comes close to me. An old lady brushes past me as she reaches around me for a pack of bacon, I'm waiting at the end of one of the aisles and I'm in the way and I burst into a set of new tears. I beg my mum to let me out of the shop, but she yells at me for asking and I'm trapped, I can't escape and I feel like I'm going to explode.

"I don't want to go!" I scream in retaliation, I'm now completely unaware of my surroundings and unable to keep all the emotions inside. "You can't make me, and I *won't* go!" There is nothing that my pleading and yelling and crying will do, it's obvious I'm going.

*   *   *

On the day of my lesson at the new tennis club, I am silent, completely mute. My parents think it's ridiculous that I'm behaving in such a manner, but how can they not see that this is the worst thing in the world to me right now. I'm scared and I want to beg them one last time to not make me go but I can't use my words again and I know it won't achieve anything anyway. I watched Jesus get down on his knees and beg God for something once and that worked out well for him, so I tried the same with my grandma once whilst we were shopping but she walked off and when I opened my eyes there was another woman in front of me, it was all very embarrassing. It's fair to say I will never get into a prayer position on the floor again outside of my own home.

I arrive at the new tennis center bag in hand, containing my rackets, balls and water bottle. I slam the car door and walk begrudgingly to the courts, where there are five teenagers, much older than me, warming up. I have memories of swimming, where all the children are older than me but not as good as me and they're all resentful and nasty towards me. Why do my parents not understand that I don't want to keep having the same experiences over and over again?

Tony introduces me to the group, giving me a proud smile; none of them smile at me. I know what they're thinking, I'm a small, little girl who's going to be rubbish and drag the team down. Everyone buddies up and I'm left standing on my own, Tony pairs me up with a tall, dark-haired girl called Olivia and her friend, Jake, a brown-haired, tall boy with a nice face. It's obvious they are friends and are annoyed that they've been put with the little girl. After a while of warming up, Tony instructs us all to take a quick break and drink some water.

"You're really good." Olivia smiles at me, she's friendly but she doesn't want to be my friend. Sometimes, that's worse than people being nasty, they don't dislike me, but they also don't want to be my friend. I feel so lonely around sporty people; I never quite manage to fit in, always on the edge of the circle and never invited to join in without adult instruction. I never get invited to play with the other children at the tennis club, no one ever phones me to ask me to come and practice with them and I never call them because I know they don't want to. Everyone has their group of friends at tennis, and I never fit into them, so I practice by myself, hoping that someone will invite me into their game.

At the end of the session, Tony asks my parents if they will drop off Jake and Olivia at their house up the road, which they are more than happy to do. All three of us cram into the back and Olivia sits in the middle, sliding a little closer to Jake than me, which it's fine by me. It's only a few minutes journey and they thank my parents for the lift as they climb out the car and grab their bags from the boot. They wave bye to me and head in the direction of their houses, as they walk together, they smile and laugh and enjoy being around each other and my body aches for the same feeling. I always get on better with boys and I just want a friend like Olivia has, who I can laugh and smile with and be myself with, not pretend to be a character in my book. I make it my mission to find a friend like Jake, who gets me, wants to spend time with me and be my best friend.

10
WASHING MACHINE WOES & THE START OF SELF-ADVOCACY

January 2022

Furiously, my fingers press in my dad's phone contact into my mobile and sit in a stream of tears, waiting for the call to connect. He answers the phone after five rings with a chirpy 'hello' until he realises I'm crying on the other end.
"Aww sweetheart, what's the matter?" He coos.

"What's wrong, Harry?" I can hear mum's voice in the background; she picks up on anything and everything, her ears like a hawk in our house.

"I'm just shit at everything, I can never get anything right" I cry in exasperation and explain the details of the morning, whilst making my breakfast. All the emotion and stress had made me forget to eat and I realised suddenly, I was immensely hungry. Six weeks ago, Jack and mine's washing machine broke, and we spent a week trying to find someone to fix it, to which we were advised to get a new one. We spent the next week sitting on that and not looking at washing machines, a week later I started to look on Curry's, my parents helped me find one because decisions are too difficult for me. That washer spent the next week in my shopping basket, by the time I had got round to ordering it, it had gone out of stock. I spent another week finding a similar one and finally, finally ordered it.

Today, it turned up ready for installation and recycle of my old washer, however when the man turned up, he told me I had an integrated washer and had ordered a non-integrated washer. Back to square one and crying in exasperation, I phoned my parents for support.

"It's because both you and Jack are the same, usually one person knows a bit more about DIY!" Mum tries to reassure me. Whilst cooking breakfast, I thought I'd turned the grill on but actually I've turned the oven on because I once again, can't shift my attention between two tasks.

"No, not just that, *everything*, I can't do anything right." The tears have started again, "I can't look after a bloody house!"

"It's all a learning process," she laughs kindly.

"You just need to ring Curry's and see if they will exchange it, if not then we'll find another way to put the hinges on" my dad says, but the integrated one is more expensive, and the installation looks like it's another seventy pounds from the link my dad has sent me.

It's then I realise my hot cross buns have burnt again while they've been in the grill and the cheese has melted so much it looks none-existent. That's it I can't take any more, I'm in full-blown meltdown now and I put the phone down on my parents. I can see the garden ruined from the storm last week that we still haven't got around to clearing up, there's food on the floor from where the dog has messily eaten his breakfast and I've stress eaten a Dairy Milk bar now. *Is this something neurotypical people can deal with?* I ask myself. *Or is this something they just don't have to deal with?* I can feel complete rage filling me up from my feet to my head and I throw the hot cross buns across the kitchen, screaming and hitting myself on the leg, like I used to do when I was younger. I've not felt this overwhelmed for years, everything feels too big, and I just want to stop the loudness of the feelings in any way that I can. I don't hate myself; I hate the feelings that are choking me and making me unable to process logical thought or emotion. I want to be away from everyone and everything, in the dark, in a cupboard where no one can find me, and the feelings are contained.

Being an adult just seems too hard in this moment, as a child I relied so much on my parents to help me time-manage, remember and break down tasks into more manageable parts. When I got stuck in the middle of a task, my parents would prompt me what I was doing and what I needed to do next. I don't have the luxury of this support anymore and I really didn't know how much I needed it to be a functioning adult. Jack has taken responsibility for the bills and paying the mortgage because otherwise deadlines would constantly be missed. It still takes me weeks to book doctor's appointments and order prescriptions, just generally looking after my physical health is a challenge, never mind all the things I need to do to support my mental health.

As my rage settles and logical thought begins, it strikes me for the first time since my diagnosis that this is my disability, I am disabled, and I don't think I even realised that until just now. I've felt lazy and unproductive for most of my adult life, as soon as I moved out for university, I realised how lazy I was. But really, I was never lazy I just had executive function difficulties where initiating and finishing tasks is challenging, time estimation and management are challenging, remembering things is challenging. Maybe it's okay that these things are difficult for me, maybe it's okay that I need other people to support me, maybe I'm not a failure. This feels like an epiphany, I've spent all this time trying my hardest to be independent and get my act together but the best thing to do is ask for support from people and accept their reminders and strategies instead of getting angry at them for babying me. All this time I thought it was so important for me to learn to live independently from my parents and do everything for myself when really, I should have been learning how to ask for and accept the support I always have and always will need.

I think about all the neurodivergent children right now in schools who are taught to grow up and be self-sufficient and independent, just like I was, and how this ridiculous message is damaging their self-esteem. I tried so hard to do things by myself because I was made to believe I was burdening other people if I didn't, really, I was burdening my parents when I rejected their support. Why couldn't someone have told me that it was okay for me to ask when I needed help? That I could lean on someone when I needed support to regulate my emotions or remind myself of a doctors' appointment? There and then I make a vow to myself to teach every child that I can that it's not weak to need support, independence is not the only thing we're striving for, it's also about autonomy and the skills to self-advocate.

*   *   *

It's been a few weeks since my meltdown over the washing machine and I've just about recovered. I've been mulling over my revelation ever since, acknowledging each day the tasks I find difficult and always have and seeing them through a new lens. Today, I have decided I'm going to ask for help with things that my executive function puts barriers between and I'm not going to be disappointed in myself for it. I pull into my parents' driveway and take a deep breath, *there is no shame in asking for support,* I tell myself silently and push open their front door.

"Hello." I mumble as I enter the house, mum immediately knows my mood is low and thinks her words over before she says them, giving a sympathetic facial expression, along with a smile.

"Hi Harry, why don't you come and sit with us whilst we have our breakfast?" She pats the seat next to her as dad enters the room. Looks like dad won't be having a seat at the breakfast bar with his bacon sandwich now. It's not hard for dad to judge my state of mind either, as he notices my lack of eye contact and closed-off body language, so he does little to protest his offered up seat. Instead of speaking, he strides to me and touches my cheek, smiling as I look towards him. Putting my bum on the buffet I take another deep breath and do what I came here to do.

"I need some help." I mutter, eyes fixed to the table in front of me, "As you know I haven't been great recently and I've really struggled with getting stuff done. I've had loads of cards I need to send to people, and I've just not got around to it."

"Okay, so what do you want us to do?" Mum asks, with a tone that indicates she's happy I'm finally letting her help me get myself organised. For years, she's tried to remind me both her and dad are there to help me when things get tough.

"Well, I've bought the cards and I've written them, but I just can't get around to looking up the addresses." I give a slight smile, which they replicate. I'm massively downplaying this, four months ago my friend had a baby, I bought a present and card, wrapped and wrote the card and despite her living only ten minutes away I haven't given them to her yet. Her baby now no longer fits into the newborn size and I'm too embarrassed to go around with a 'new baby' card now, even if I did find the will to start the task of driving there.

"No problem, why don't you tell me how many stamps you need and then we'll walk to the postbox together?"

Dad suggests.

"Well, it's a little harder than that." I admit shyly, why is this so hard? I feel so ashamed that I can't even do the most basic of things that my parents seem to think I can do. "I need help to look up with addresses on my phone and to keep on the task and to go and get the stamps and then to stick them on and then remember to take them when we go to the postbox." Although they both smile and agree to help me, my dad's face betrays him. He's shocked and it shows, he looks ashen with the realisation that life is so much harder for me than he anticipated. Never would anyone believe that a girl who smashed all of her GCSEs, A Levels and graduated from university, who is now a woman making such quick advancements in her career so young would ever need someone to sit down and help her write addresses on cards.

"Okay, where do you keep the addresses? Let's sit down and do this." He smiles warmly and I know there's no shame from my dad, just shock that he didn't realise that his daughter's disability was in fact, a disabling disability. I feel my body instantly relax as he sits beside me talking me through the steps and keeping me on track. My brain resists every minute of it but in this moment, at least I know I have help with the rest and it helps me to feel like I'll be successful from now on.

WHAT I WISH YOU KNEW

11
JACKET POTATOES & GENERAL NIGMO BIFFY

2004

"Today, I want you to write an introduction to yourself." Mrs Berry announces to the class. "I want you to write about what you look like, what interests, what you like and don't like and your personality."

I always find these tasks difficult because I always get told that I'm giving too many facts and not any information on my thoughts or how it makes me feel. I don't know how I feel so I would rather talk about what things look like and are like. I put pen to paper and immediately start to scroll through the facts about myself in my head:

My name is Harry Jayne Richardson. I am nine years old (that is one of my favourite numbers). I have brown hair and ginger and blonde in it as well. My eyes are a blue and greeny colour. I have an amount of freckles on my face. My body is small and thin.

My interests are sport (tennis, hockey, cricket, javelin, and taking my dog for a walk twice a day and other things too). I gamble on snails. I write stories. I sing and I love horse riding. I hate ballet and Maths and mushrooms.

My mum and dad think I am sometimes a terror my dad thinks I am sometimes a tomboy because I spend more time playing with boys' toys and army tanks and the action men go to war. My brother always shares the PlayStation and thinks I can be a little bit nutty sometimes.

My friends thinks I can act daft sometimes, they describe me as: funny, friendly and kind and Maisie thinks I'm different.

Mrs Berry commends me for quickly finishing my piece, with lovely, neat handwriting and allows me some time to continue reading my book 'Cat and the Stinkwater War'. The book is my favourite ever thing and I sometimes re-read parts of it because it is just too enjoyable, I love cats and I love the cat characters in the book. My favourite character is General Nigmo Biffy, I would like to be more like him because he is brave, and everyone does what he tells them to. In the playground, I pretend to be Nigmo and tell everyone the story, giving them different characters in the book to play, which everyone really enjoys. I'm often making up stories in the playground for everyone to play, the teachers say I have a very good imagination but sometimes I get a bit lost in it, whatever that means.

Mrs Berry has finished marking my work and hands it back to me with a smile. Anxiously, I rifle through the pages seeking some confirmation that I did the right thing. On my page of writing, she has underlined the word 'different' in a red pen and I wonder what that means. Does it mean that she agrees I am different? Does it mean that it's a bad thing? Is it a word I shouldn't write in my book? Is it emphasis on different? I don't like that she underlined that word, she could have underlined friendly or funny or kind and that would have been nice, but she didn't she underlined 'different'. I must be 'different'.

My teachers always write that I do really well in my writing and I'm very good at setting a story, but that sometimes they are a bit muddled, and they ask me to write them again but this time make it easier for other people to understand what I mean. I don't really understand this, because my stories are really easy for me to understand and writing them again makes me really upset. When mum and dad come for parents' evening, they always say that I've done really well, and I behave really well at school and I'm really eager to learn. They also say I have strengths in imaginative writing and English but struggle a bit with understanding Maths when I have to do new types of sums. I always make silly mistakes like not reading the question properly and sometimes I need help to understand what a question is asking me to do. Mum and dad always tell me the same thing every year that sometimes I can daydream a bit and don't always respond when people talk to me and that I'm very shy and never ask for help when I can't do things.

I get a little bit annoyed that they keep saying the same things because no one ever helps me to do better they just expect me to start doing these things myself. I don't know exactly what someone else is asking me to do because they're not very clear, I don't even realise I'm being spoken to sometimes and it makes adults think I'm rude, but I just don't hear them. I also really don't know how and when and why to ask for help, teachers are always talking and helping other people and they get angry with me if I interrupt them, so I just stay quiet. School is confusing sometimes.

My best friend at school is Linda, she's a lot like me in looks and we often get told we're like sisters, brown hair, slight build and a smatter of freckles. I like Linda because I know when she's my friend and when she isn't, she tells me when I've made her mad and will stick up for me when other people are being nasty. All the adults call Linda 'fiery' but I don't really know what that means, I guess it's because she's very loud and knows what she wants and gets what she wants, sometimes I wish I was a little bit more like her. I feel comfortable with her because I don't have to make decisions and talk lots because Linda does most of the talking and bossing everyone about. It makes me happy when I don't get pressured to make a choice and talk a lot, so with Linda I feel great.

Sometimes though, she can be very bossy and loud and shouts at me if I won't do what she says and falls out with me. When we give her a ride to school, some mornings she pushes her feet into the seat I'm sitting in, and it gives me the hot feelings and I start to cry because I want to tell her to stop. Mum asks me why I don't stand up to Linda when she's being mean and tell her that I don't like things. I've told her I don't know how to and it gives me the worry feelings and I would rather just ignore it. Mum says I need to get a little bit better at standing up for myself because when I go to big school it will be harder than it is at my school now.

The thing I like most about Linda is that she likes to play the same games as me. Some days we play imaginary places, where I have a bar called Nigmo Bar and she has a restaurant called Gizmo Restaurant and everyone else comes to join in our game. Lucy tries to join in and change it all, she's made herself a hotel called Lizmo Hotel and that makes me angry because it's mine and Linda's game and she's ruining it all by putting a silly hotel where it shouldn't be. Linda tells her to go away, which is nice because I don't have to. Other days we practice for our band called Dark Puppy, we sing a lot of Atomic Kitten and take it in turns to sing different parts like the girls in the band, I like that there's boundaries and other people don't try to sing at the same time as me because then I can't concentrate on the words. We are trying to look for a third member of our band and a few of the girls in Linda's year have tried out but none of them seem to understand that they can't sing over the top of us, which gets really annoying.

I'm going to Linda's house for a sleepover after school today and I'm really excited, this morning I even did lots of happy jumping. I never like to sleep at other people's houses, but I think I can manage at her house because I've been there lots. Mum and dad will be there too because they're friends with Linda's mum and dad, I call them Aunty Lou and Uncle Graham. I feel happy that my parents will be there because then if something goes wrong, I can just run downstairs and sit with them instead.

I skip up the drive to school and see Linda and her mum waiting at the top by the stairs to our classroom. Linda looks strange, she has puffy eyes like I get when I've been crying, I hope that she's okay because I don't want it to ruin our sleepover. As we get closer, I can see that Linda is angry with her mum, she's standing away from her and every time Aunty Lou talks she moves further away and scrunches her face up. That's when I notice Linda's had a haircut and she looks really different, that must be why she's mad, I would be mad if my mum made me cut my hair like that, especially when I hate having my hair cut. The hairdresser talks to me too much and too loudly and I panic that mummy will leave and I'll have to talk to the silly lady who talks about everything and nothing at the same time, when all I really want to do is hide under the thin blanket they put over me and not say a word. Mum often answers the hairdresser's questions for me and that makes me feel good. The hairdresser also touches my ears too often, she says it's because they stick out so much, but I just think she wants to make me angry because every time the comb touches the top of them it makes me really, really hot and I want to scream at her to stop.

"Look at my silly hair!" Linda yells as we approach her, "She's made me cut a silly fringe and it looks silly." She gestures towards Aunty Lou in anger.

"Oh shhh, you look fine. It was getting like rat's tails." Aunty Lou says with no sympathy, it's obvious she's heard too much about it. Mum says the same thing about my hair being like rat's tails when it gets long and I don't understand, it looks nothing like rat's tails, they're all pink and bald. I guess that it means it gets scruffy because she said Scruffy's hair looks like rat's tails too.

We walk into school, leaving our mums at the end of the steps. Linda keeps talking about her silly hair and I zone out, worrying that she's going to be in a bad mood for our sleepover and it's going to ruin things. We walk past the kitchen on our way to our classrooms and I see Mrs Peters setting up for our toast snack and it makes me gag. I already tried to eat some breakfast this morning and had to hold my breath while eating the rest of the buttered bread, I don't think I can cope with looking at more bread after that. I start to feel hot. Linda jabs me in the side with her elbow.

"Oi, did you not hear? We've got a film to watch tonight." Linda talks about a film called Bridge to Terribithia and I start to worry, I don't like to watch new films without seeing the cover of the DVD because it's got to look right, or I'll get upset. I hope I like the look of the DVD when I see it. We split into our separate classrooms, Linda is in the year below me, but I wish I was in that class because I don't feel as mature as the girls in my class.

Grace and Maisie were the only other girls in my class last year, they both loved horses and were really good friends and I always felt like I bugged them if I tried to hang around with them. I so desperately wanted to be friends with them, but every time I tried Grace would make me feel silly and say mean things to me. When Grace wasn't there Maisie would be my friend and we'd play horses together, I enjoyed days when Grace wasn't in school because Maisie was really nice to me then. Mostly, I spend time with the boys in my class and the year below, they're much easier to get along with and don't make fun of me in the same way or leave me out on purpose. Will is in the same year as Linda and has been my friend for a very long time, we play tennis together and he really struggles when he loses matches too. We go to the tennis club together and I think he feels left out as well, but it's okay because we're left out together. On a Tuesday night he comes over to my house and we have jacket potatoes with tuna, sweetcorn and cheese, mum always makes the best jacket potatoes and Will says they're much better than the ones his mum makes. He eats the jacket potatoes with his hands instead of cutlery and mum looks shocked every time he does it. Last time he came over, when she picked me up from tennis, she told me that I mustn't copy how he eats his jacket potatoes. She doesn't need to worry I don't like it when I get food on my hands, it's gross.

Ben, James and Peter are my friends too, but James left to go to another school nearby at the start of year six. Ben is a little boy, who is smaller than me in height but broad at the same time, he reminds me of a thimble, he has a cheeky smile and he's moving to Florida after we finish school in summer. Peter is my friend, but he annoys me too because he keeps proposing to me and trying to kiss me and I don't like people touching me, never mind people trying to touch me on the lips. He likes Barbies and pink things, and I don't, I like to play football with the boys in the year below and Ben, I'm not good with my feet because I can't move them in the right way but I'm good at catching balls so I stay in goal with my gloves on so that the football doesn't hurt my fingers when I catch it.

There are only three of us in year six and we join on to year five to do our work most days. Everyone keeps saying that they're going to close the school down and our year will be the last year six and everyone will have to find different schools for the next year. I'm sad that the school is closing because it has been my home for such a long time, but it also doesn't matter because I won't be here anymore. I'm going to a high school and mum and dad are arranging some visits for me when I get my year six test score results. I'm really nervous about changing schools and don't like to think about it too much. Linda has been visiting some schools in the last few weeks, but she says all of them are rubbish compared to Sunflowers.

When I get home from school, mum makes me some tea before we go to Linda's house. Mum and dad are eating at Linda's but I get worried about not liking the food, so I always eat before I go somewhere, just in case. We set off, my overnight bag packed with Scruffy and my favourite pyjamas. My excitement has started to turn to worry, and I nibble at the edges of jumper until the sleeves are soggy, I never sleep over at people's houses.

Last year all the year sixes and year fives got the opportunity to go on an overnight trip, which everyone was really excited for, but me. I did not want to go on the trip; mum and dad knew that I wouldn't go before I even said it.

"No way, I can't go and stay somewhere overnight." I said, "Can I please just go for the day?"

"Yes of course, sweetheart." Dad says and strokes my hair; maybe he does understand how hard these things for me. When the day came for the trip, I was so worried about it that I got a migraine and had to stay in bed all day. I could hear mum on the phone to my grandma whilst I was in bed.

"No, she's not gone mum, she's in bed with a migraine again." Mum says over the phone, and then she listens to what grandma says in return.

"No, I know mum, she just gets herself worked up about these things and gets sick."

"Yes, we tried to get her to stay overnight but sometimes it's just not worth it mum, she just gets so upset." Mum has tried to explain to my grandparents lots of times that things can be really difficult for me, but they don't seem to understand, they tell mum that I need to learn and that she should leave me in bed when I won't get up and should make me eat whatever she puts on the table to eat. Mum gets really upset about that sometimes because she feels like she is trying her best but other people think she's not doing the right thing to help me; I can hear her talking to dad about it sometimes. I don't understand why I find going on trips and sleepovers so difficult, it just makes me really worried every single day before it happens and then I get so wound up that my head hurts and I end up in bed not able to move or speak, sometimes I'm sick too.

Linda's house is only ten minutes from mine, next to a reservoir that we walk Basil at often. I like her house and her bedroom because she has a bunk bed and I really want one of those. Alex has a bunk bed in our house, but he won't let me sleep on the top bunk when he comes to stay because I must sleep in my own room and leave my brother to have his space, as dad says.

After a few hours of playing, me, Linda and her little brother Harry are sent to bed and we settle down to watch Bridge to Terribithia, Linda cuddles her Dalmatian teddy and falls asleep halfway through the film, but I can't sleep when there's noise and it doesn't feel right to turn the TV off when it's not mine. I hate it when other people fall asleep before me, I don't like to be the last one to do anything, and it makes my stomach feel sick. At the end of the film, I find out the main character girl is actually dead and it's confusing and sad and tears roll down my face. I get big emotions when I watch films and sometimes adverts of the TV too, I don't even realise why I'm crying at it sometimes.

Unsettled feelings start and I want to go home with my mum and dad, I hope I'm not too late, I really do not like sleeping at other people's houses, but I can't move out of this bed it's like my legs and arms won't work and I'm trapped. Linda's still sleeping as mum steps into the room to say good night, I wrap my arms around her neck as she leans down to kiss my head.

"Please can I come home with you mummy?" I

whisper. She smiles and nods picking me up in her arms and carries me, half in between sleep and being awake. She knows she doesn't need to check if I'm sure, she knows what I need because she's the best mum. As we get downstairs mum whispers to dad that he needs to go and get my things from upstairs, I think he thinks I'm asleep as he ruffles my hair.

"It's already all packed up," he laughs, "I knew she'd be coming home with us but I'm glad she tried." I cuddle closer into mum's shoulder and fall into a deep slumber, not waking up until the next morning.

*   *   *

"Where did you go? You didn't even say goodbye." Linda asks me on Monday morning.

"Sorry, I didn't feel very well so mum and dad took me home. I didn't want to wake you." Please don't be mad; please don't be mad, I think. Linda shakes her head and rolls her eyes.

"You never stay over." She shrugs, accepting that's just me and moves on. "I have something to tell you, I've found a new school and I'm going to move there in a couple of weeks. It's a really cool school but I'm going to miss you." She grins really widely, and I can tell how excited she is, but she doesn't seem to see how unhappy I feel. My friend is going to another school, just like James did and I can't do anything to stop all these changes, I feel completely out of control and don't know what to do. What will school be like without Linda? She annoys me but she sticks up for me and plays games with me. I start to cry as soon as we part ways and I rush to the toilet to hide my hot, damp cheeks from everyone.

12
INFODUMPING WITH THE ILLUSTRATOR

April 2022

Naomi is the most wonderful person I know, without doubt. She is a friend that I've always truly cherished and been able to be myself around, ever since I met her four years ago at my first Speech and Language Therapist job. There are many times that Naomi and I have met up for dog walks to have informal therapy sessions, speaking about the problems we're having and giving each other a listening ear and advice, where we can. She's been there through many things for me and vice versa, we always know that we can rely on each other even when we don't get around to texting each other back.

I so look forward to my chats with Naomi, it doesn't matter the topic, it's just never hard work and we've been meeting and chatting recently to work on a book together, the words on my end and the illustrations on hers. A few weeks ago, Naomi texted me to tell me she thought she might have ADHD, to which I replied a very quick 'yes, I'm glad you've figured it out' followed by a conversation into the early hours of the morning because once we start sometimes, we just can't stop, even when sleep is required to get to work and do a decent job the next day.

A few days after, she had sent me a picture of a quote 'your soul is attracted to people the same way flowers are attracted to the sun, surround yourself only with those who want to see you grow.' We often send each other cute little quotes about our friendship and so I take time to send her a message to check in on her, after the realisation she could have ADHD, along with a quote I'd seen online: 'stop gas lighting yourself with the narrative that you're lazy when you're really exhausted AF from just surviving moment to moment.' I relate to this so much from my own experiences of ADHD.

She replies promptly, talking about how she's processing her new perspective and speaks of lots of the same things that are currently going on in my brain. I press the voice note button.

"Ergh, I just *get* you." I start, laughing and I talk about how I'm processing the situation, "Sometimes I just feel like such a bad partner and have felt like such a bad daughter over the years because I come home from work or school and just be completely unable to speak to people and need to be by myself. I'm just in bad burnout at the minute and I just feel like I'm not there and can't connect with other people. I've felt so bad for everyone close to me because I've just not been there for conversations or anything. It's been so hard. I'm also really sorry for my slow response time, but I know we said we'd never apologise for that, so I'm taking back that apology, sorry for apologizing!" I start to tell her about my hyperfixation states and completely info dump without care or concern. I add to the end of the messages: 'P.S. hope you're ok x '.

"Let's just acknowledge how super prompt my response time is, like I'm super proud of myself!" She laughs on a voice note, "Yay! Quick response time, but yeah don't apologise, you know it's okay. Also, infodumping is great, infodump away." She begins to talk about her memory issues with ADHD and all of the things that I relate to on so many levels and it just feels like home. This includes sitting in our cars when we get home for absolutely ages and even when we need a wee won't move and will just sit there and wiggle because our brains can't move on and reboot in order for us to physically move.

We talk and talk for hours about our processing of our neurodivergence and how it's making us think about life differently, without concern about how long our voice notes are. I start to notice that my voice is quiet, then sometimes really loud, with an excitable tone and my hands start to flap in uncontrollable ways. There's a massive smile on my face and I realise that this is what it feels like to connect with someone who is also neurodivergent. There is no one else in my life who I can just voice note all of my thoughts and infodump and not worry about them getting bored or telling me to stop going on about the same thing and it just feels like the biggest relief I've ever experienced.

Many times, I've heard autistic people on Instagram and Twitter talking about 'finding your neurokin' and how important it is. It wasn't until this point right here that I realised that this is a feeling I've never experienced and it's all because I don't mix with neurodivergent people. After my realisation I open another voice note to Naomi.

"I just need to say that I genuinely think you are the person I unmask with the most, and like always have done, like this is me, this is normal me, I don't even try and speak at an average pace or anything, or intonation. I'm literally flapping now, I'm stimming because I'm excited and this is really strange but also really great. Also, I kind of want to cry because it's really nice because I don't do that with anyone else and yay. So, I think I might go and cry now." We share the emotional moment, agreeing that we both feel this amazing connection that allows us to just be who we are.

"I've started doing work on my identity and I'm going to be really upset saying this, I didn't know who I was, like genuinely what I liked. I would make myself listen to music that other people liked and convince myself that I should like that. I've done that all of my life since being tiny, did what other people wanted me to do, I liked what other people wanted me to like, I behaved how other people wanted me to behave and dressed like other people wanted me to dress. I have no idea who I am and that is big, it's traumatic. I'm slowly trying to figure out exactly who I am, which parts are me and which parts are the mask. I wrote down all the bad things that people have said about me and what I've believed about myself and so much of it is rubbish because everything that's been said is because of autism and ADHD. It's just miscommunication and misinterpretation and that sucks. I've just spent my whole life listening to people's negative options of me and it's not something I should have changed or be made to feel like I had to change, that was just me and it wasn't negative. I wasn't being blunt or impolite it was just my communication style.

I'm just overwhelmed and so glad I've got you. Like I

love so many of my friends, but I can't unmask around them right now. I might not ever get there, I'm not sure I'll ever feel comfortable enough to and I really wish that was not the case, but it is, but at least I've got you. Just yay, I love you."

"Ahhh I just love ya." Naomi replies and as the conversation draws to an end, we decide to put our phones away so that we can get on with our days because if we carry on in our excited states, we will both have an extraordinary come down and we're both on the verge of being mute and in need of a nap after all of the infodumping.

I put my phone out of my reach and go to make my lunch because I've hyperfixated to the point that I've forgotten to eat again. Despite the distraction from everyday life, it feels like life is different now, I don't feel quite so alone in this strange reality that I now find myself in. I'm not alone, there are other people out there who are like me and don't find me annoying or too much or want me to act certain ways and Naomi is one of them. I love my parents and Jack, but they will never be okay with me sitting there and talking their ears off about neurodiversity and mental health and all my advocacy work for hours on end. They appreciate how passionate I am about my passions and encourage me with it all but there comes a point where they want me to stop talking about it.

Before my diagnosis, Jack told me that he found it frustrating that I only speak about certain things, which is usually around my work and mental health. Jack enjoys talking about politics and history and general world affairs and often I'm very shut off to this line of conversation because it's too general. Sometimes, there are historical events and politics that I find interesting, and I will speak about but a lot of the world issues and things that happened in the past are too abstract for me because I'm not experiencing them and it's hard for me to understand and connect with the events.

At times, I call my dad to read him elements of my book and ask him questions about my childhood so I can patch up the memories and although he always answers the phone and listens attentively, sometimes I can call him five times a day and I can tell it's draining for him. My mum, who is very like me can struggle to listen to me infodumping because the things I am interested in are very far from her own and nowadays we have very different perspectives and viewpoints. Sometimes, when we have a healthy discussion, it can get heated because we're both so alike in that we like to thoroughly get our opinions across and we have to be right. I don't phone my mum to tell her about work or my book because I know that's not something she wants to speak about but all the other events in my life, she's only a phone call away.

There are many myths about autistic people, one of them being that we are unaware of others' perspectives and needs, and whilst I do struggle to understand people's perspectives, I am hyperaware of non-verbal cues, like facial expression and body language. This means that I immediately know as soon as someone is checking out of our conversation and has enough of what I am saying. Over the years, my family has tried to fain interest in many of my passions but unfortunately, I know exactly what they're thinking by looking at their faces and posture. Being aware of these subtle cues can be a burden because I so desperately want to talk about the things that interest me, they are held within my mind, so tightly and the more I don't let them out the more they build up. Instead of saying them out loud to people I have to write them down in blog posts and in my journals but somehow it is never enough. It's not enough to find these interests interesting by myself; I want to share them with the people I care about. Now I know that I have someone in my life that I can do this without judgment or lack of interest.

I wish Naomi had always been in my life, I wish she were around when I was a little girl who wanted so desperately to talk about all of the things she was learning and reading and writing. I wish there had been someone like Naomi in my childhood years, my teenage years, university, just to show me that I could share my excitements and infodump to my heart's content. I think back to all of those years I suppressed talking about my interests in favour of my friend's boyfriend, or the sleepover that was happening that weekend.

I'm thankful that I found psychology in my A-Levels because I could spend hours on my essays, writing and writing about my findings and volunteering answers and opinions in the classroom. I just wish I'd had someone to share this with instead of writing it on a piece of paper for my teachers to read.

I have never, in my twenty-six years felt so myself than I do in this present moment, after infodumping with Naomi. My body, my mind and my personality feel free and unrestrained. All of my life, until this point right here that's how I've felt: restrained, unable to move, speak and do as I wished. I didn't realise how much I'd suppressed, blocked out and neglected until this very moment. It is almost as if the weight of expectations and pressure of conformity have lifted from my shoulders and been cast aside. I'm beginning to know who I am and I really, really like my authentic self.

13
THE HOLE IN THE HEDGE

2001

The sun is so warm today; it streams down onto my back and makes me feel all floppy. I don't feel great when it's warm, it's like my limbs don't want to work and I'm so tired in the sun. Mummy waddles over to me in her flip flops that fit between her toes, she's tried to get me to wear those type of flip flops before and I scream when they slot in between my toes. I can't cope with things or people touching my toes, it makes them feel all out of place and I can't get them back into the right position. She holds me in place whilst attempting to rub sun cream onto my shoulders; I squirm underneath her hands and try to slip away. I hate it when people touch me like that, especially with strong smelling goo, I just want to get away, but mummy keeps rubbing and rubbing, I'm starting to feel angry now. The smell and the feel of the sun cream lingers on me for what feels like hours afterwards and I want to rub it all off and never put it on again.

Daddy is cutting the hedge and I don't want to go near to him because the sound vibrates my head and makes it feel like it's going to explode. At a comfortable distance from the noise, I dip my toes in the paddling pool and look up into the sky, watching the clouds and making them into shapes, a bunny, a crocodile, a table. The noise stops and I turn to watch daddy, who is now piling up the parts of the hedge he has chopped off and putting them into black bags, I hope he doesn't ask me to come and help because my body feels too weak from the sun. That's when I spot blonde hair through the hedge, there's a little girl running around, all her long hair trailing behind her in the air and immediately I know I want to be her friend. I like being by myself sometimes, but I get lonely when Alex isn't around and mummy and daddy don't want to play my games, it would be nice to have a best friend. Mummy notices me staring through the gaps in the hedge.

"Why don't you go and say hello?" She asks me tentatively; we both know I won't be so brave but that doesn't stop her from encouraging me. Daddy pokes his head through a bigger gap in the hedge to introduce himself to the neighbours over the wall.

"Hi there," he waves at the man on the other side. "Just cutting my hedge for the first time in a long time, we've never even seen you before!" The man on the other side laughs.

"Dave," the brown-haired man with a square face and big eyebrows offers my dad his hand to shake, "this is my wife Kim, Alfie and Anna." He gestures to a lady with mousey hair and a warm smile, an older boy who's skinny, tall and shaggy-haired and the little girl with long, blonde hair. Daddy introduces me and mummy and we all gather round the gap in the hedge to talk to the family over the wall. I hide behind mummy, peering nervously around her to eye up my potential new friend.

Anna is the same age as me; she's a dancer and goes to a

junior school down the road. I like Anna, she has a kind smile and she's shy too, partially hiding behind her mummy like I am. The man called Dave asks if I want to come over and play with the kids, I'm a little nervous but I really want to make friends with my neighbour so I agree. Daddy lifts me over the wall into their garden, it's not as big as ours but it has a bee enclosure and vegetables around one of the edges.

Me and Anna play in her garden all day, playing tig and hide and seek, I found an excellent spot just behind some big fur trees at the far side of the garden farthest away from our house. From my hidden spot behind the tree, I can see my parents resting in their sun chairs, my mum in her fancy, frilly orange shorts and dad in his hedge-cutting outfit, they look happy, smiling and laughing, enjoying not having to entertain me for a while. I feel proud in that moment, hidden behind the tree, not that I haven't been found by my new play pal, but that I've explored in someone else's garden and me being brave has made me a new friend.

Later, Anna invites me to come and look at her dolls and I'm so excited that my new friend wants to show me something of hers because I want to show her all of my things too.

2005

Anna and I play together most days, when the weather is sunny we play hide and seek in the garden and sometimes Alfie joins in too. I like Alfie, he's cool, and I like the music he plays, he seems to like me too, just as I am. I like spending time with them both because I know I can be my silly self with them, and they don't think I'm weird like everyone else does.

Anna is now well-acquainted with Scruffy and Snowy, when we go out, she looks after Snowy and I carry Scruffy. Anna reminds me of Snowy, she's pretty and girly. We're complete opposites me and Anna, she wears pink dresses and dainty shoes and I wear my shorts, boy's t-shirts and trainers; she dances in a tutu at ballet, and I play tennis and rough and tumble with the boys at school. Despite all our differences, we do everything together and I know we will be best friends forever. I wish I could have hair like her, it's long and beautiful and I wish I could be more like her, everyone likes her, and all the adults think she's cute and well-behaved. Anna does everything that girls should do, her mum and dad must be so proud of her. Alex likes Anna too, he really liked meeting her, but he said that she doesn't do the things that I do and she's not as cool as me because she doesn't play video games and water fight. I like that Alex likes me best and just as I am.

Dad has built us a ladder to climb over the wall and cut the hedge in an arch so that we can easily fit through without branches scratching us, my parents are very happy that I'm spending lots of time with Anna and that I have a friend. Mum likes to invite Anna whenever we go to places like the beach and that makes me happy, it feels like she is my sister, and I don't feel so lonely anymore. When Anna's parents take us places, I feel safe because I know I have my best friend with me and I don't feel so frightened in new places because we can talk to each other in our secret language. I even went to see Anna in her dance show, sitting with her mum and Alfie in the third row of the audience, I was so proud to be her best friend.

I sometimes sleep over at Anna's house now, I feel okay about this because I know that my house is only over the wall and if I need to, I can get out of bed, climb over the wall and go back into my house. Anna's bedroom is right at the top of her house in the attic, and you have to climb lots of steep stairs to get to it, she has a window that opens wide in the roof and I like to hang out of it and watch people walking past on the road, the fresh air feels lovely on my face.

Anna has lots of ribbons in her room that hang from the walls, they're all for dancing, just like my medals for swimming and tennis. There's lots of space in Anna's room and she has a big bed for us to sleep in when I stay over. I don't like it when she falls asleep first because I don't want to be on my own somewhere that's not my bedroom, so sometimes I kick her and poke her so that she wakes up and I can try to fall asleep first. One time, she told me that if I whispered 'Mars bar' in her ear she would wake up, I tried it a few times, but she never woke up and I didn't like that, she lied to me. When I wake up in Anna's house, I feel worried because I don't like the things that they eat for breakfast and I panic that they will make me eat something strange again.

All Anna's family don't eat meat, she's a vegetarian and they eat funny sausages called Quorn, they got me to try one once when they had a BBQ and I really didn't like it, it felt slippery and wet in a dry bread bun but mummy said if other people give me food I have to eat it, so ate a bit even though I felt sick and threw the rest in the bush next to me. I like being at Anna's house, but I really wish they would let me eat normal food that doesn't make me feel sick whilst I'm there.

Once, Kim took Anna and I off for the day to a shopping center and we went into an antiques shop, which was just incredible. It wasn't like regular shops, with the bright lights and pops of colour everywhere, the space was dark, and everything was spread out into different categories. We made a game of pointing out all of the shiniest objects and scouring the aisles for the most expensive product, it really was fun. Right at the back of the shop was a clump of old music gear, which Kim was talking to the owner about with interest, Anna's dad is a musician and Alfie is learning to play the guitar, so she was looking for some equipment.

In the clump of items stood two pairs of shoes, one

being some white boots that Anna's eyes set on and the other being a pair of Union Jack platform boots, all red, blue and white, my favourite mix of colours with a little glitter on the sides. In sync, we rushed over to inspect the boots, both being our sizes, it was fate. Excitedly, we approached Kim, the boots clutched to our chests, grins and eyes wide.

"Please, please, please can we get these boots mum? They're so pretty." Anna begged.

"I think they're a bit old for you both girls, they're high heels." Kim dismissed our requests and proceeded to buy the music equipment. The car journey home consisted of us both sulking and those boots have been on my mind ever since.

*   *   *

We're on the way to Centre Parks in the car, mum and dad are sitting in the front, dad is driving as usual, and Anna and I are sitting in the back with her bag of things between us. I feel a little bit squished but it's okay because the excitement of spending the whole weekend with my best friend outweighs everything. We are going for the weekend with some of the kids from my school that I'm not really friends with, but mum and dad are friends with their parents. I'm excited to spend time with Anna but the closer we get to the lodge the more other feelings start to emerge and my racing thoughts become harder to push to the back of my mind.

Whilst Anna talks about her week my thoughts wonder to all of the possibilities the trip could bring and the realisation sinks in that I'm not sure what to expect when we get there, I've never been to Centre Parks and I don't know if the picture I have in my head will fit. I become quiet, unable to process language because of all my worries and thoughts, mum and dad speak in place of my silence so that I can figure out all of the questions in my head in peace. Anna asks if she can sing because she's been having singing lessons and mum agrees we would all like to hear it. I suddenly feel cross, Anna is good at all the things I'm not good at, I can't sing, and I really wish I could, I feel very cross with how hot I feel, the fact that Anna is having a nicer time with my parents than I am and that I'm going to a new place. I stare out the window and ignore everyone as they praise Anna for her singing, she continues a little longer and dad snaps.

"Okay, okay, that's enough Anna," he says, trying to cover his ears while gripping the steering wheel, his knuckles going all white. Silence at last, this feels more comfortable.

When we arrive at Centre Parks, we drive up a long, single-track road lined with fur trees. As we approach a barrier dad stops the car and talks to a strange looking man with an uneven moustache, it annoys me, I hate when things aren't symmetrical. Wiggly moustache man checks our booking receipts and allows us through the barriers, dad drives further along the road, and we pass long lane after long lane of wooden cabins, all looking the same. Finally, after much déjà vu we hit a dirt track and squeeze through a wall of looming fur trees, emerging at two big cabins, next to each other surrounded by trees, I recognise Ang and Lee as soon as we pull up.

Ang is mum's best friend, her and her husband, Alan have two boys, Lee and Jonny, who are both annoying and like to wind me up. We are staying in a cabin with them, unfortunately. The other cabin has Lynn and Tim and their children Georgie and Sam, who are both younger than me, and Kathy and Jim and their children, Lucy and Little Jim, who are also both younger than me. Lee is the oldest boy, at two years older than Anna and me. Mum and dad said I was allowed to bring Anna with me because I don't really get on with the other children, they talk about things I don't want to talk about, and they don't stick to the rules of my games.

Ang envelops mum in a big hug, and I start to worry that I'm going to be expected to hug everyone too. Why do adults feel the need to squish their bodies against mine? I only like it when mum and dad and sometimes Alex and grandma give me hugs, everyone else squishes me and holds on to me for too long. I escape the cuddles by following Lee into our cabin for a tour. It's very grand with a log-burning fire in the living room and sky-high windows that spread all across the front of the cabin. Everything is wood and autumnal colours, I like that there's no busyness like in grandma and grandpa's house, and it makes me feel calm. Lee and Ang show us to the bedrooms on the top floor and Anna and I settle into our shared room, which I was happy about, I just want to spend time the two of us and not all these other people, it feels too much, they are all so noisy together. Sometimes I ask mum to be a bit quieter because she speaks so loudly but she just rolls her eyes at me and tells me to stop being silly. Dad and me have our own private joke when she answers the phone that she shouts so loud they could hear her without the need for the phone.

*   *   *

The weekend is a blur of activities, bike riding, horse riding, and swimming and so much more, usually it would have been a dream of a weekend for me, all that activity, but it isn't. I don't like having to be around all these people all of the time, some of them are really difficult to talk to and I don't want to play with them, I want to be with mum and dad because I can sit next to them and feel safe. Everyone really likes Anna, especially Lucy and Georgie, they stick to her like she's glue, and I don't get any time with her apart from when we go to bed, it's not fair, she's my friend not theirs.

I guess it's not their fault, everyone likes Anna because she's the perfect friend and daughter; she never does silly things or gets in trouble or says the wrong words. When she makes jokes, everyone laughs and they all like to join in with her dancing, for the first time I feel alone with Anna and it makes me cry. I'm not speaking much this weekend and that's unusual when I'm around my best friend.

Today, we're going to Santa's grotto and then ice skating in the evening, I hope I get what I want from Santa this year, Christmas really excites me. As we arrive at the grotto, everyone gets really giddy, all the girls squeal and hug each other and talk about the Barbies they are going to ask for this year. I hug myself; I don't want to get involved in this weird celebration, I don't know how to do that and I'm worried about going into a space that's got lots of people and I don't know what's in there. I shuffle over to where Lee, Jonny and Sam are standing, they're far less fussy about going in the grotto, they show their excitement in ways I can understand, like smiling.

Suddenly, Anna grabs my hand and leads me into the grotto, anyone else and I would pull my hand away and shake my hand around to get rid of the feeling, but this feels okay because she's my best friend and I'm just happy that she'd rather hold my hand than Lucy and Georgie's. This gesture tells me that I'm still her best friend too. For a minute, it feels okay to enter the grotto, I just keep my eyes on Anna's fur-lined coat in front of me and her long blonde hair that floats down past her waist, it's okay, I'm just playing in my garden at home I tell myself.

The end of the snow-trodden path stops abruptly, and we all huddle behind a large door blocked by two elves. The tall, balding elf mutters that we have to wait until it's our turn to enter the room where Santa is, but don't want to wait here, everyone is piled up in a small space and I hate it, I feel all squished and squashed and like my body is in a vice, the thing that dad uses in the garage that he winds up and squashes things in. I don't want to be in a vice, I don't want to be here, I want to be at home in my bed with Scruffy so I can cry, rock myself and put a blanket over my head to shut out the world around me. I close my eyes and imagine I'm somewhere else, I can't speak, and everyone is talking all at once in anticipation of what Santa will look like and who's going to get the best present from him. I say nothing, I hardly breathe, it feels too hot in this small space.

Finally, the door opens and we're all released into a slightly bigger room, Santa does not expect to see seven children behind the door, looking shocked and laughs.

"Come on in everyone!" He laughs in the jolly way I expected Santa to laugh. He looks at me and I turn my head away, I don't want this man to look at me, I don't know him and although he brings me nice presents every year he's scaring me because I can't see his face to know what he's thinking behind his big beard, glasses and hat. It's like when I see Mickey Mouse or anyone dressed up in a costume, I don't like that I can't see their face, it makes me want to scream and run away. How do I know what someone is saying and thinking and feeling and is going to do if I can't see their face or watch their mouth move? It's impossible to be okay when I can't find any clues and I just have to understand their words.

Santa asks me what I want, and I turn my face away, I can't speak to him because every time I look at him I get this enormous wave of fuzzy feelings. Anna tells him that I'm hoping for a puppy and Santa laughs a big belly laugh, I hate the sound. An elf interrupts us, asking us to gather around Santa for a picture, I take this as my opportunity to move away from the white-haired, fat man, edging to the corner of the room. Away from Santa's eyeline, I stay stationery, my fingers curled into my fists, squeezing my thumbs as tight as I can. The camera flashes and I realise I didn't smile; I couldn't move my face in the right way, Anna has her arm round Georgie and I want to be as far away from all these children as possible.

"Why are you ignoring me?" Anna asks me as we exit the grotto. I shrug and look away from her, not being able to find my words just yet. She walks ahead of me with Georgie and Lucy, looking upset and annoyed.

*   *   *

I still haven't properly found my words as we approach the ice-skating rink, everyone gets fitted for their skates and mum tells me to be careful on the ice because I don't want to hurt myself or I can't play tennis. That thought worries me. I want to ask mum for help as she leans down to tie up my laces, but I just place my hands on her shoulders, unable to ask, so I just enjoy the feeling of my mum underneath my fingernail-lacerated palms. *Take me home please*, I think but can't say. She looks up at me, still on her knees and scans my face for a moment, without saying a word she puts her hand on my face and smiles a knowing smile, she knows how difficult this weekend is I think in that moment.

I don't want to go on the ice, I want to stay with mum, and everyone is already on there, Anna is helping Georgie to stand upright and I don't want to interrupt them, I'll just feel like a nuisance if I do. I stand on the edge of the ice, waiting for someone to invite me over but no one does, so I stay rooted on the spot.

"Go on!" Says mum, giving me a gentle nudge. Anna searches the crowd at the entrance of the rink, calling over and waving me towards her as she spots me, but my feet won't move, it seems too big to get involved in everyone else's play.

"Harry, what is wrong with you?" Mummy turns me around to face her, she looks upset with me, but I don't understand why. I don't know what is wrong with me, I just feel a bit stuck. "We've brought your friend with us for the weekend, and you've just ignored her the whole time. Sort yourself out and stop being so silly, we've had to look after poor Anna all weekend because you've been like this."

I realise suddenly that mum doesn't understand like I thought she did just moments ago. I don't know what to say, I don't mean to be a pain, I just get stuck and can't talk or do what everyone else does. I really try to be like everyone else but sometimes my brain doesn't let me, and I feel too tired to do anything. I just want to be like everyone else, why can't I just be normal like mum and dad and Anna want me to be? I ruin everything and I've ruined my best friend's holiday and probably everyone else's. I just wish I wasn't me.

*   *   *

Two weeks later…

It's Christmas day and I'm so very excited! As soon as I open my eyes, I smile my biggest grin and wriggle around under the bed covers. I really, really love Christmas day. I hate the build up to Christmas, everyone talks about it too early and I hate all the flashing lights that everyone puts up outside their houses, I asked dad not to put them up at our house. But there's so much that's good about Christmas that the horrible lights and commotion doesn't matter all that much. I love eating chocolate each morning before breakfast, I love the big dinners with lots of mash potato and gravy, I love that we do a school play and I get to do lines and make my parents and grandparents proud.

Christmas Day is the best day because the same thing happens every year, I go downstairs straight into the snug that has hundreds of presents to unwrap, Santa and his reindeers have always eaten their treats, there's always fairy dust around the fireplace and we eat the same food that I know is extra tasty because dad makes it just as I like it. I get to open just one present before my grandparents arrive at ten o'clock for our breakfast, every year they all have a bacon sandwich and because it's a special day I try to eat it too. This year I choose to open a squishy present first, it sits on top of a big box and inside is a teddy, a black and white cat that looks like the one on Postman Pat, I call it Jess, it's the best thing ever. I always wish for another teddy because they are my favourite things in the world, they're so soft and make me feel calm. I always want to get one wherever we go anywhere but mum and dad say I have too many now.

Grandma and grandpa come over at exactly ten o'clock with the same sacks of presents, I know immediately which sack is mine and which is mum and dad's. When they come in, they hug me tightly before giving me the sack of presents and I set about organising everyone's presents into different piles and shaking them all to try to figure out what is in them. This year, dad has made sausage and bacon sandwiches for breakfast and because it's such a good day I don't mind how fatty the bacon is or how dry the bread feels, nothing can ruin this day. We start opening presents straight after breakfast and I decide who gets which present, everyone has to have a present in their hands and everyone has to open them at the same time. I ask mum to give me the worst presents first and end with the best presents because otherwise I feel disappointed, but she forgets what she's wrapped, just like she does every year. I wish she made a list of what is in each one like I do, so that she remembers.

I'm always opening my presents way after everyone else has finished because I have the most and everyone turns their focus to me and what I'm doing, I love this part of the day most because I love it when things are just about me, and I don't have to share. I'm sometimes sad that Alex doesn't come to our house on Christmas Day, but I don't think I'd like to share this special day with him and for him to have some of everyone's attention. Everyone is always in such a good mood on Christmas Day, and we never fall out, even mum and grandpa get on and he gives her a hug and kiss and I like it when they are nice to each other, I hate it when they argue, and they do that a lot but I don't understand why. Dad gives me extra hugs and kisses on Christmas Day, and we all go for a walk at lunchtime, grandma and grandpa hold hands, which they only do on special occasions, it makes me smile that everyone is happy and together as I walk in between mum and dad, holding both their hands in my gloves.

Dad makes the best Christmas dinner; the turkey is always really big and my grandparents take home some in a Tupperware every year. On Boxing Day, dad always makes a curry, which is really nice and has raisins in it; I love the raisins and knowing what I'm going to be eating. Dad makes the best mash too, it's not like the mash grandma makes that's lumpy, his has lots of butter and milk in it and it's all creamy and smooth and I like to suck it to the roof of my mouth. No one even tells me off for eating weirdly or sitting in the wrong way at the kitchen table on Christmas Day.

In the afternoon, I organise all my opened presents into lines and group them into their different categories: toys, clothes, puzzles and other. I play with each one of them for a little bit before moving on to the next, everything feels so new and exciting and I have to show everyone what I have and re-group them over and over again. I can't wait to share my new things with Anna; she's going to want to play with all of them.

Christmas Day is so magical, and I know how much my family loves me on a day like today, they're all so happy and give me lots of hugs. It feels like I can be a lot more me on this special day and everyone accepts it without telling me off or ordering me around. I feel like a normal kid today because everyone is so happy around me and I wish they could always be like this but I know I make things difficult most of the time for everyone so they can't be. But that doesn't matter right now, because today I go to sleep with the biggest smile on my face, cuddled up with Scruffy, Snowy and Jess.

14
WHAT WOULD A DIAGNOSIS MEAN TO YOU?

December 2021

I'm in the depths of the internet, I'm not sure there's anything else I can read on female autism at this point, but I just need more, I need more information. I'm aware that I'm driving my parents and Jack to distraction because it's all I talk about but then it's all I can think about. I've decided not to tell anyone else because I need to keep this to myself until I know for sure that I'm autistic, though I'm sure I'm autistic. I don't think I've ever yearned for something so much in my life, I don't just want a diagnosis, I need it because then my life will just all make sense.

I text my therapist, Claire to request an appointment with her because I know that speaking to her is the confirmation that I need and I already know exactly what she's going to say. She texts back quickly with an appointment for the following week and now it's just a waiting game, one antagonising wait that I'm going to fill with more late-night research.

Christmas is coming around quickly, and I've become more aware this year of why I've always found this time of year tricky but also immensely exciting. I've always loved spending Christmas day with my family and doing the same, predictable thing each year, with a rigid routine and a present system that I'm in control of, much to everyone's aggravation. It's only this year that I understand for the first time why I don't like Christmas outside of December.

Firstly, who thought it was a good idea to start Christmas advertisements and songs and celebrations in October? I can't be excited for long periods of time because then it turns into anxiety of not being able to keep up the positive emotions long enough, of having to fake it if I don't feel happy on the actual celebration day and not being able to be good for over a month so that Santa will come and visit me, it's a lot of stress. I also have always hated

Christmas lights, especially the flashing ones and the multi-coloured ones; they're a sensory nightmare and give me migraines. I really liked Santa, but the idea of having to sit on an unfamiliar man's knee, with his body touching my body and use my voice to ask for presents has always been too much. And then, worst of all the Christmas songs, which are just plain irritating, it's all fake joy and I hate it. Christmas songs are fine in December but not before that, it just feels all wrong!

I know that everyone gets the January Blues after Christmas and New Year celebrations are over but that's especially poignant for me, having feelings of elation along with intensely long periods of socialising just makes me crash for a couple of months and sometimes I even wish that Christmas didn't happen in my house so that I wouldn't have to experience the depression following it all.

I love receiving gifts at Christmas but struggle with opening them with anyone but my family because the facial expressions and tones I have to use to appear grateful is draining and I don't like the unpredictability of people potentially giving me things I don't understand. I totally get now why I hate getting any kind of toiletries because it's likely I'll hate the strong smell and the feel of things like lotions.

Despite my love for receiving presents from my family, the very best part about Christmas is giving people their presents because that's my way of showing my love to someone, not words and affection, but showing them that I really get them and know them by giving thoughtful gifts. I get so excited about people opening their presents that by the end of the day I'm a wreck and go into shutdown because the emotions have been too much. The problem is, I'm always disappointed with other people's reactions, they never quite get excited enough about their presents in comparison to the reaction I'd imagined in my head. I hope that each time I won't let their lack of reaction affect me too much, but it always does.

I'm completely aware that people are very thankful and appreciative of the gift, but it never matches my own joy. When someone gets me a present that tells me that they get me, it gives me a feeling of intense joy and appreciation all over my body, I feel heard, understood and seen. Earlier this summer, for my birthday my high school friends had given me some gifts and the best thing was a pack of chocolate in the shape of dumbbells, because they know I love the gym so much. I couldn't explain with words how much the gift meant to me and spent the next weeks going in the cupboard just to look at them and smile. I didn't eat the chocolates for over a month and that's some restraint for me!

I guess I could say that gift giving and receiving is a special interest because of the excitement it brings me and the intense research and focus I put in around people's birthdays and Christmas. I love to celebrate other people and show them they are appreciated because I struggle to show them in alternative ways. I guess allistic people (those who aren't autistic) don't experience the same joy from this and so I'll add that to my list of reasons I think I'm autistic.

*   *   *

My therapy appointment comes around after a slow week of Christmas excitement and celebration at work. I'm a ball of nerves but also can't stop smiling, it feels like I'm transitioning between anxiety and excitement on a secondly basis and the internal feelings are very confusing, they don't appear to connect with my facial expressions, which I've lost control of. The call connects and I see Claire's familiar, friendly face on the screen and instantly I know this was just what I needed.

"So, how are things?" She gets straight to the point, knowing that chit-chat makes my skin crawl and I'd run away if I could. Internally, I thank her for knowing me so well and saving me from the discomfort.

"Erm, it's been a strange month, I have something I want to pass by you, and I think I already know what you're going to say but I've been doing all this research and I've come to a conclusion and I know that it might be out of the blue." I'm rambling because it feels scary to get to the point and I want to justify my reasoning. "So, I think I might be autistic." The word lingers in the air for a moment. This is the first time those words have left my mouth and I realise that they are indeed what I needed to hear myself say for the confirmation that this is what I am seriously thinking. The words make all of the thoughts and guesses real and they feel like a fact. Claire smiles, her wide, knowing smile and lifts her hands in the air.

"Ahhh, you've finally arrived." She laughs and the relief is overwhelming, I'm not making this up, this person who gets me most in the world sees it too and so many memories of our sessions come rushing back to me. Claire saying that she thought a family member of mine might be autistic, asking me to confirm that I found eye contact challenging, asking me if I often felt like people just don't get me.

"I know you've given me signs all along, but I just don't think I was ready to listen to them or go there until now. And just hearing you say that is probably the biggest relief of my life."

"Yes, so you noticed the hints then." She smiles a wry smile, "I think I probably recognised you were autistic after the first or second session, just out of interest would you like me to have told you?" I consider this for a moment, knowing that Claire will allow me time to process the questions without interjection and there's no need to meet her eyes whilst I think, which helps me.

"No, I don't think so, I don't think I was ready for that, and I needed to get to that myself, if that makes sense? I'm not sure I would have accepted it before now."

"Just what I thought. So how do you feel about being autistic and where would you like to go from here?"

"I feel like so much relief has just washed over me, all the guilt I've held for what I put my parents through and always feeling like I was such a bad daughter has started to dissipate and I feel a whole lot lighter." I start to cry, which is unusual for even my therapy sessions. I find it challenging to cry in front of anyone apart from my immediate family and Jack. My friend at university once slapped me across the face whilst drunk because she thought it unfair that she cried in front of me, and I never showed the slightest emotion in return. I still like to remind her of this out of character action, to which she always tells me to stop reminding her whilst hiding her face behind her hands in mock shame.

"I just always knew that I was different, and I feel so upset for the younger version of myself who went through so much rubbish without support or understanding. I feel so sorry for my parents who were completely lost and without knowledge of how to support me. There's a lot of emotions that I don't really understand right now but I do know that I feel relief and happiness in that I've finally started to understand myself. This feels like the start of a brand-new journey and I guess the next step is to get an official diagnosis."

"What would a diagnosis mean for you?"

"I feel like I need a full confirmation of it and be able to tell people that this is the reason I am like I am. I feel like it will really help me understand who I am and feel more comfortable in my identity. The biggest thing for me is being able to talk to my students at work about it and connect with them and be a role model to show them that autism can be a positive part of your identity, because already it does feel positive to me."

"Well, that sounds like an excellent reason for a

diagnosis! Let's get you some information for a referral then."

15
THE MUSHROOM FIASCO

2003

"Quiero, un atun y tomate por favour." Dad requests in staggered words and a half-hearted Spanish accent from the lady at the bakery counter. We've gone to visit my grandparents who live in the south of Spain, like we do every summer. I know how to ask for a tuna and tomato pasty now because that's what I have for breakfast, lunch and snack every day in Spain. We visit the same supermarket and all I want is my pasty and some Milka chocolate, oh and of course grandpa's special biscuits, which have chocolate on top of a plain biscuit. I like to nibble the chocolate off the edges first and grandpa tells me off for being like a squirrel.

"John, why is she not in the Squirrels group instead of Beavers?" He asked my dad as I nibbled my way through a second special biscuit one afternoon this summer. He was clearly exasperated by my table manners; he wouldn't be the first and he certainly won't be the last. He was referring to my group in Brownies, I don't like Brownies, I wish I didn't have to go and be part of the silly Beavers anyway. They make you do all sorts of team building activities and I would much rather go off and play alone with my one friend in Brownies – Jessica.

We exit the shop, just down the road from grandma and grandpa Spain's house, the white, green and red carrier bags hanging from dad's arms. Unlike mum he never asks me to carry the shopping and just allows me to focus on tucking into my sixteenth pasty of the week. We've only been here seven days.

"You can ask for the pasties yourself Harry, you know enough Spanish to do it." He looks at me sympathetically, knowing it's not the language barrier that means I can't ask for things. I like going to the shop with grandpa or dad because when I go with mum, she gets all nervous about asking for things because she doesn't know Spanish and sometimes, she accidentally uses French, which means I have to ask for things when mum is there.

"I know." I say, shrugging and eating the edges of the pasty, it tastes strange today like its dry and the tuna and tomato don't feel right together anymore, I stop eating it and tuck it behind my legs, so dad thinks I've eaten it. It's lunchtime and I'm on my break from tennis camp, which starts at 8am and finishes at 3pm, with an hour break for lunch. All the other kids hang out together around the pool, but I return to mum and dad each day for some rest from talking and trying hard to make friends with no success, I don't fit in with any of them, on or off the courts. We're walking back to where mum is sunbathing at the pool, her favourite thing to do on holiday; I don't understand why she likes it so much. I get too warm too quickly and would rather sit under my towel than feel the sun burn me; it makes my head feel too light. People often ask if I went on holiday with mum and dad because I come back the same colour, whilst they're sporting golden tans.

We walk through the tennis center, along the cobbled paths between the tennis courts and I seize my opportunity, throwing my pastry into the bare trees along the edge of the netting between the courts. Dad turns, spotting no pasty in my hand.

"Where's the pasty?" He glares at me, analysing me for signs of mischievousness and comes to a stop just after the place I've thrown the pasty.

"Ate it." I blurt out, staring at the floor. Sometimes dad lets me off with not eating things, he doesn't get as worried or annoyed as mum and bargains with me about how much I can bear to eat. I think maybe he understands it a bit more because he would rather starve than eat sauces or mushy peas. Grandpa at home gets really cross with dad when he won't eat his mushy peas because they're the only thing grandpa can cook and he's very proud of them.

"Seriously, where is it?" He groans, peeking into the carrier bag I'm holding, before scanning the floor behind me, with his gaze settling on the bushes behind me. "Have you thrown it in the bushes?"

"No." I lie, trying to push past him as he spots the brown and red evidence in the bush.

"Then what's that?" He points, he's smirking. I know that he's trying to remain annoyed, but he really wants to burst out laughing, he's so close to laughing and I burst out into giggles, at which point he concedes and joins in with them.

"This isn't funny!" He tries to change his tone but the ridiculousness of me trying to hide a half-eaten pasty in the bushes is just too much to resist a good laugh and in the moment, I know we have agreed this is something we don't need to share with mum. We have an unspoken agreement, if he tells mum about my disappearing pasty he knows I will tell her he laughed about it and then we'll both be in trouble. He offers me some bread in replacement, and I take it willingly, thankful that I have such an excellent dad.

* * *

Tennis camp is great, I love it! I love tiring myself out on the court, proving all of the coaches that I will work as hard as I can. I love their acknowledgement of my hard work and I always win 'Most Valuable Player' in the awards at the end of the week because I will work harder than everyone else no matter how small and quiet I may be. I like spending time with the coaches more than the kids, the kids are confusing and all snigger when I do things wrong, making jokes that I just don't get. The coaches are kind and partner up with me when none of the kids want to.

Every evening dad puts me a bottle of water in the freezer and packs up my tennis equipment, as the sun rises in the morning, he takes the bottle out the freezer and walks me down to the tennis centre, whilst mum and my grandparents are still sleeping. I find it difficult to part from dad when we get there because I know I'm going to have to try and find someone to speak to and partner up with when he leaves and that is something I hate doing. I'm awkward and move in weird ways when I don't feel comfortable, my face and body don't match what I say or how I feel, and they all notice it. As soon as dad leaves, I spend as much time as possible fiddling around in my bag and drinking some water to avoid having to speak to the other kids.

When I'm on the court it's fine, I can just relax and play the sport I know I'm good at, I can make friends when there's not all of the uncertainty of what to say and do and there's structure. I'm a different person on the court, I'm comfortable and confident and I demand respect, sometimes I might come across as assertive, but that's not really who I am when the game ends and I have to shake hands with someone, which feels wrong and unsettling. I know how to congratulate someone on their win or commiserate them on their loss, because I just use the same words I use every time, but if they want to talk about something else after the match there are no boundaries and I panic, not sure what to say. That's when people realise they don't want to be my friends and we part ways so that they can spend time with people who feel more comfortable to be around and have a conversation with.

I spend the unstructured times in the tennis camp watching everyone else chatting and laughing with so much ease and wonder what they are doing and am I not, watching helps me to understand what I should be doing around people my age. Coaches think I'm hard working because I just want to get on with the next match, the next drill, the next task but it's not just because I enjoy the exercise, I also want to escape the socialising that leaves me stuck and unable to function.

Every morning that tennis camp is on I feel this horrible feeling in my belly, and I can't eat anything because I feel I might be sick, dad is okay with this because he knows if he tries to force me to eat I just get more upset. I dread turning up at the tennis club and walking into a space with all those people, unsure of what to do and who to speak to, so I always want us to be late so that I can just get stuck straight into the game with no greetings. I wish I could take away all of the talking and eye contact and making friends part of the camp, I just wish I could automatically have friends without trying and that we could just play tennis all day without the breaks.

Sometimes, I don't want to go to tennis camp because the talking to people and trying so hard to fit in feels too big and I get frightened of people avoiding me and making fun of me again. It seems that whenever I do make a friend they aren't in the same group as me because they aren't as good and then I get stuck with all the extra confident and older kids who find me odd. I love tennis but some days it doesn't feel worth it to have to put myself through all the difficult bits. Mum and dad don't understand why I panic and cry about going because I just can't explain what is wrong.

In the afternoons at tennis camp, we do an hour of fitness, which means doing things like cross country, sprints, sand sprints, and circuits; this is the worst part of the day. Today is our last day at camp and so they make it extra hard, and I think I might faint. In the height of heat my body starts to feel floppy and everyone gathers together with all of the different coaches, just when I was starting to feel more comfortable in my smaller group. I would rather skip this part of the day, I think about running off, I'm so quiet, would anyone even realise?

I feel so much better when I've done the activities though and I always feel proud that I got over the worst part of the day. When we finish, everyone rushes over to the pool and jumps in; some dive, some bomb and others simply sit on the side. I'm happy to skulk away whilst no one notices and find the safety of my parents, who are lounging by the side of the pool, books in hand. I have no one I'm friends with to say goodbye to and no one notices my absence.

"How was it?" Dad jumps up, seeing me approach. I show him the MVP t-shirt that I won with a broad smile spreading across my face. "Wow, Most Valuable Player! You're a little superstar, chicken." Mum's head rises next to him to see what's going on and she gives me a big smile and a thumbs up before looking across at all the other children then back at me. I know in an instant what she is thinking: *why is Harry over here with us when all the other children from tennis camp are together and having fun?* She doesn't say anything but we both know it's obvious I didn't fit in, yet again. I wonder if she's wondering what's wrong with me because there must be something, I'm always the only one on my own. I'm not like the other kids, is she wishing I were?

I shrug off the thoughts and scuttle over to my lounger, the triumphant feeling returning as I put on my MVP shirt and collect up my goggles, ready for my favourite part of the day – my coin hunt. Mum makes me wear a T-shirt in the pool because my little shoulders burn so easily and today I do not object because at the end of a long day of people and demands it is time for me to switch off and play my calming activity that I must do each day. I strip off my tennis shorts and enter the water with a grin, time to decompress. My game is simple, predictable and repetitive, which brings me intense comfort; I dive to the bottom of the pool and search for coins that people have dropped, last summer I got a whole twenty-four euros and thirty cents.

The feeling of disappearing from view of everyone's eyes and judgement is like nothing else and I wish deeply that I could just turn into a mermaid from one of my books, so that I could breathe under water and stay below the surface in the safety of quiet and solitude for as long as I want. Breaking the surface of the water for air is the worst part of the game and I try to hold my breath for as long as I can manage to savor the moment. I ask dad to keep an eye on my pile of coins on the side of the pool and he does a good job, warding off anyone who dares go near to my treasure, whilst I just enjoy the pressure of the water on top of me and the softened, echoed sounds under the surface.

It's an escape, no one knows I'm here at the bottom of the pool, moving between their legs, undetected able to watch everyone else from a distance without being detected and judged. I transition from pool to pool, completing my routine in each of the three pools and I feel disappointment when it's over, I've been under the water for an hour and now it's time to go back to reality and for the weird feeling in my body to start. I exit the water and run over the dry, horrible flagstones that feel like they're stripping my feet of moisture, into my towel that feels wrong, dry and scratchy underneath my fingers, and there they are, my raisin fingers, which I lick frantically. It's not good enough, the sensation of all three sensory assaults gives me the shivers and I get up and run on the spot in my sandals, shaking my hands and sticking out my tongue. Dad looks towards me, confused by the random movements.

"What are you doing?" He looks towards my flapping hands, that my tongue is frantically licking and my kicking feet.

"Everything feels all wrong, like dry and nasty and I feel all uncomfortable." I don't think those words really explain how I feel and sensing his confusion I try to settle on my lounger, putting the towel over my body so that I lick my fingers in the privacy of my own space. Poking out of the edge of the towel, my toes are scrunched up as tight as I can to get rid of the dry feelings. I like to spend most of my day by the pool like this, underneath the safety of my towel, being watched by no one and in my space safe, where I can read my book and get lost in the world that's created by the words on the page. It's difficult to read when things are moving about around me and the sun feels too warm on my skin and bright in my eyes.

When I'm not under my towel, I put on my red, rimmed sunglasses and watch everyone around the pool, taking in everything they do. I like wearing sunglasses because no one knows I'm watching them and I have learnt that the more I stare, the more people get freaked out. Grandpa got freaked out this morning when I came down for my breakfast, entering the room and scanning it with my eyes, getting myself used to my setting and processing everything. Dad said grandpa was angry with me for being rude to him because he said 'good morning' to me and I didn't respond, but I didn't hear him or even know he was there until after I had processed the room. Sometimes, it's as if my ears don't work and I switch them off when I'm looking at things because I can't take in information from both at once.

Here, around the pool is the perfect time to watch other girls and learn from the things they do. There's a girl, a little older than me in a crop top, pink bikini that everyone crowds around and wants to talk to, she's sat with the older teenagers and the rest of the kids from kid's club who all sit on the opposite side of the pool to us, in the 'cool' section. I wouldn't dare to approach any of them because they all know each other already. The pink bikini girl is splashing some of the younger kids with water and whispering things in her friend's ears, making them laugh. I wonder what she's saying and what's so funny, I wish I could do that, but people never laugh at me like that, a lot of the time they don't even get my jokes, especially the girls. A lot of the time the adults get my jokes and laugh at me but they're not who I'm supposed to be making friends with.

I watch how the pink bikini girl moves, the way she flicks her long hair and the way she stands, with her hands on her hips, always smiling and looking towards people when she speaks to them. She's not like me, facing away, crossing my arms and hiding behind other people or shrinking myself instead of standing up straight. This is how I need to be when I go back to England, I need to be like pink bikini girl who looks at people when they talk, her shoulders upright and standing on the dry flagstones without jumping up and down and licking her fingers. I bet she doesn't even get raisin fingers.

I set about on my mission; I will stand on these flagstones without being weird just like pink bikini girl. Flicking my little legs over the side of the lounger, I stand to my feet, slide off my sandals and plant my toes and heels on the hot, dry flagstone next to the lounger. The feeling is unbearable, I want to move onto my tiptoes and then back onto my heels, but I don't, I stay fixed on the spot, not crunching up my feet, my face or my fingers, just looking normal. A few seconds into the mission, my hands begin to form fists around my fingers to stop myself from licking them and I can feel my nails digging into my palms but somehow the feel of my nails piercing my skin helps, because it feels like a relief from the feeling of the flagstones beneath my feet.

After a while, I retire back to the lounger and throw my towel back over my head, immediately throwing it back off, pink bikini girl does not put her towel over her head like a weirdo. I look down at my hands as I uncurl my fists and release my nails from my palms, seeing the indent they have made, tiny, curved moons carved into my hands all pink and sore. Quickly, I hide them away from mum and dad's sight. My hands might hurt but I did it and I can keep being like the pink bikini girl, as long as I try my hardest.

*　　　　　　　*　　　　　　　*

On our last night in Spain, grandpa makes us his classic paella as he states 'every Spanish resident should be able to make'. He cooks it on the barbecue with just his apron, shorts and sandals on and from the balcony below I can hear him requesting my help and I leap up with so much enthusiasm that I startle mum, who can't get me to do anything helpful at home. I'm not keen to know how to make a paella because I don't like cooking, but I'll do anything to spend just a little bit of one-to-one time with my granddad. I finally feel useful to him. We carry the ingredients down the steps; the flagstones warm on my toes as I tiptoe across them, carefully avoiding the tiny ants that dash up and down in neat lines.

In the mornings when we stay at grandma and grandpa's house, I like to sit and watch the ants, sometimes I place things in their way to see what they will do and where they will walk to. I don't like to touch them though, that would be gross!

Grandpa barks orders at me for where to put ingredients and I fumble over the pans and bowls, trying eagerly to get everything right, following his gestures rather than his confusing words. Mum approaches with two hats, both for chefs, I take it gladly and place it on my mass of curls, I love wearing hats everyone knows that. Grandpa gestures for me to place his hat on his bald and shiny head, filled with freckles, leaning down to my height, unable to use his hands for the oven-mitts and utensils in them. I pull the chef hat over his head and right over his eyes, giggling as he stumbles and attempts to pull it up with his mitted hands.

There are so many ingredients that go into the pan and I busy myself clearing away the bowls and utensils he discards to the side, taken in by his knowledge of what goes in when, for how long and with which spices. It's all magical. Grandpa lets me stir the paella, slowly but just enough so that the rice doesn't stick to the bottom of the pan. I can hear everyone on the balcony above chattering and laughing and am glad I'm in the safety of a task, not having to make chit-chat. It's so nice to spend some time with grandpa on my own, learning from him and having something to focus on rather than making sure I answer his questions correctly and say the right things. I find that I really like the escape that cooking brings, I'm sad when it's over but happy that I get to eat something I've co-produced.

We ascend the stairs, grandpa carefully carrying the massive paella bowl over to the rest of the family, all of them waiting with anticipation and hungry bellies. Everyone applauds as we approach, and I feel a sense of triumph as grandpa announces his sous-chef was fantastic and plants a kiss on the top of my curly-haired head. Grandpa isn't one for gestures of affection and he very rarely gives me credit for things I've achieved, it feels great to have his attention, affection and acknowledgment.

Fred, the lizard that lives in grandpa's wall makes an appearance at the smell of paella and scuttles towards grandpa, who smiles and greets him. Fred is the best thing about this house and sometimes I wish I could be Fred instead of me. He comes and goes as he pleases, can run away and hide in the wall whenever he wants and doesn't get shouted at for watching everyone else and not joining in. He doesn't have to talk; he just uses his eyes and everyone loves him just for that. Grandpa wafts him away from the paella and he returns to his crack in the rock, deflated.

Now, I just want to sit next to dad and lap up his attention for being so good at cooking and doing what grandpa expected of me. He ruffles my hair as I sit on the plastic chair next to him.

"Well done chicken, I'm proud of you." He grins the grin he only saves for me. Mum serves up my portion and sits next to me helping me pick out the mushrooms and seafood out of the paella. I can't wait to tuck in; it's going to taste better than ever now that I've helped to make it.

"Jayne, that's enough" grandpa gestures for my mum to move away from my plate, "it's about time she stopped being so fussy. Harry get those eaten now will you."

"But grandpa, they taste yuck." I mutter shyly and look towards my parents for help.

"No, they don't, get it eaten. They will not kill you." His tone tells me there's no room for negotiation here and I tentatively spear the squishy mushroom, not wanting to ruin the bond we've created over cooking. It slides into my mouth as everyone holds their breath and watches, my parents unable to believe I've been convinced to even put the devil food in my mouth. The chaos the mushroom creates is instantaneous, I rise from my chair, retching. Mum rushes to grab some kitchen roll and dad springs to his feet, rubbing my back as I hover over my grandparents' balcony. The mushroom escapes in a pile of sick, falling towards the barbecue at the bottom of the garden, that just moments ago grandpa and me were huddling over. Fred slithers out of the wall to watch the commotion, blinking rapidly and looking from the mushroom splatter to me, giving me a look of sympathy. Maybe Fred gets it, I bet his grandpa isn't mean and makes him eat nasty, squishy food.

"Oh, for goodness sake!" Grandpa yells, "What on earth is the matter with you?"

"David, we've told you she can't eat mushrooms! You didn't listen, did you?" My mum stands with her hands on her hips, shaking her head at him. I run past them all into the safety of the house, up to my parent's room and assume a foetal position on the middle of their bed. Why are adults so mean? Why do they make me eat such horrible things? If I don't eat a mushroom, what is their problem? I'm not asking them to eat foods I know they don't like.

Dad sheepishly enters the room, pushing open the shutters to the bedroom, which reminds me of the old cowboy films grandpa in England watches. He settles on the bed next to me and places a gentle hand on my leg.

"Come on, sweetheart. Let's go and finish our dinner."

"I don't want to eat any more mushrooms." I look at him with pleading, wet eyes.

"You don't need to eat another thing you don't want to today. Grandpa was very mean making you eat a mushroom. I think he got what he deserved now he's got to clean up the sick." He giggles and I join in with it, it's impossible to miss out on laughing with dad. The crinkles around his eyes and his mischievous smile are too good not to share. I follow him back down to the outdoor table, taking my place safely between mum and dad, secure in the knowledge that they won't let anyone make me eat silly things again tonight.

*   *   *

It's our last day in Spain today and I'm looking forward to going back home and seeing Anna, being with all my toys and being able to be a bit more me with my grandparents not being around. The sun is shining as I make my way out of the sheer, cloth curtain and onto the patio, tiptoe walking to the wall. It's hot as I sit down and I jump up, alarmed by the burn on the back of my legs. Fred appears from the wall and greets me with a good morning tongue protrusion.

"Good morning, Fred." I whisper, not wanting to be overheard and disturbed by anyone inside. "I don't usually talk first thing in the morning, but it feels okay because I know you won't say anything back." He scuttles over to me in response and stares with his black, wide eyes, encouraging me to continue.

"It's my last day here today, Fred. We will be going back to England tomorrow morning, and I'll get to see Basil, my dog again. I think I'll miss you; I like seeing you around when we come to visit in the summer. I wish I saw you more though, you kind of come and go and I feel more comfortable being around you than I do everyone else. You don't ask me to do weird stuff, like make my bed and eat mushrooms and not lick my fingers when I've been in the pool, and not walk on my tiptoes and go and say hello to other children when I'm too frightened to.

"Oh Fred, it's all a bit much sometimes, they expect me to do so much and some days I just can't do it. It's like there's this big cloud sitting on top of me that holds me back when I should be doing what everyone else seems to do so easily. I don't really know what's wrong with me, I really want to be like everyone else and fit in, but I also just want to be just like you, Fred. You look like you have such a nice life here in the wall without anyone to disturb you. No one asks you to come out of your wall, they're just happy to see you when you do. No one expects you to perform in a certain way or change the way you are, everyone just accepts that you do Fred-like things. I just want people to accept that I do Harry-like things." Fred slithers over to my hand and places one webbed hand on my finger, I think in an effort to comfort me and tell me that he gets it. This lizard gets me more than anyone else does; I think I fit his species more than my own.

Maybe I'm a lizard, not a frog; lizards have webbed feet

too, don't they? And just as quick as it happened, it's over, Fred returns back to his place in the wall and I sit there grinning, knowing that I have an ally to return to next summer.

16
SENSORY PROFILES & STIM DANCING

January 2022

"Do you want me to do you a sensory profile?" Lizzie asks me from across the desk, now that the office has emptied of all our colleagues. She's the Occupational Therapist at work and I couldn't help but confide in her about my suspicions about being autistic. She's been all ears and super supportive, making sure I know I can talk to her about it anytime.

"Yeah, that would be great actually. It would be really good to know a bit more about what helps me. But only if you have time, I don't want to give you lots of extra work to do!" She hands me a form called a SPM (Sensory Processing Measure) and as soon as our lunch break starts, I begin filling it out, I'm desperate to know more about what makes me tick. The office is quiet, perfect for me giving the form my full attention. Everyone ventures down to the canteen to have lunch with the children but a few months ago I stopped going down, instead asking one of the team to bring me up my lunch (tuna and a jacket potato every day). It's too much to be down there in the loudness and chaos, it certainly doesn't aid digestion.

The form is a checklist of different sensory components and asks me to rate my experience from 'never' to 'always'. I'm thankful for the simple layout and specific questions.

Do you pull away from being touched lightly? Always!
Prefer to touch rather than be touched? Always!
Gag at the thought of unappealing food? Yes!
Dislike certain types of lighting? Yes!
Bothered by ordinary household sounds, such as the vacuum cleaner? Always!
Easily distracted by background noises? Always!

I finish the questionnaire quickly and look over my answers, I seem to have hit quite a lot of the 'always' and 'frequently' ratings on the questionnaire and start to doubt myself, maybe I've over-exaggerated? Having read it all through for a fifth time I decide that all of the answers are what I truly believe and hand the questionnaire back to Lizzie when she returns to the office. She tucks the form under her notebook, out of view from the rest of the eyes in the office. We get some alone time again at the end of the school day, noticing everyone has vacated the room she pulls out the completed form and sits alongside me.

"You filled that out quick, eager beaver!" She smiles, "So, basically, you've scored highly in some areas, which suggest an over responsiveness to auditory and visual stimuli and some significant over responsiveness, so a low neurological threshold, for tactile stimuli. There was also minimal but some difficulty with motor planning. Does that make sense?"

"Erm, could you explain it a little simpler for me? That's a lot of language to wrap my head around." I admit, shyly. Usually, I would have just nodded and pretended but something about my colleague makes me feel comfortable enough to be honest. She's the most free of judgement person I've ever encountered, I feel like I could recite all my life's problems to her without a care in the world of it going elsewhere. It's one of my favourite qualities in a friend.

"Well what that basically means is that touch, which is not on your terms can be significantly triggering for you, but you are okay when the touch is initiated and controlled by you. In terms of sounds, you are hyper-sensitive to these and that will cause you some distress, the same with lighting etc."

"Yeah, I can see that actually, I don't understand why I didn't realise all this sensory stuff was present before now. Thank you so much for helping me with this, it's really opened my eyes a bit to what could help."

"Just a quick question," she pauses, waiting for me to nod, "do you struggle to sleep at all?"

"Yeah, sometimes. I'm fine once I've got to sleep but can take a while to actually fall asleep when I'm stressed."

"That probably coincides with some of the sensory issues you have here. So, the best thing for you to do is have constant lighting, so black out blinds is really good for this. Also, having white noise in the background will support you to sleep too, as you'll be aware of all the little noises going on around you and outside whilst you sleep or are trying to get to sleep." Everyone from the office returns and our meeting starts and I thank her by mouthing the words and the Makaton sign, she smiles in return. Now, it's time for me to focus on my sensory system and try to work out what is going to help me regulate myself a bit better.

*   *   *

Two weeks have passed since my sensory assessment and I'm just days away from Dr Hudson giving me my results. I feel apprehensive and like I need to move. In the interview she did with my parents, they told her how as a child I always needed to be on the move, playing sports, running around, anything to keep my mind and body busy, they could never just plonk me in front of a TV like all the other kids. They even described me as a baby, roaming around my cot, unable to lie still and they had to physically hold me down for me to be able to sleep.

I can see this in my adult life, I was never able to sit through lectures at university and keeping myself still during meetings is a full-time job. I literally can't do a day without exercise; otherwise, I get all fidgety and cross and like my world is falling apart. My favourite feeling trickles all over my body, like a warm wave when I've been for a run or done a HIIT workout, the high impact just does all sorts for my mental state and physical feelings.

In the COVID-19 lockdown, when I had done my workouts for the day, because back then you could only go out once a day for exercise, I would put my headphones in and jump around to movement. Honestly, the emotions I got from doing this were magical, it was such an unequivocal feeling, and I could feel myself smiling throughout the whole experience and for hours afterwards.

The weather is terrible outside, so I turn my headphones full blast, close my bedroom door and blast my favourite workout songs. Olivia Rodrigo 'Good 4 U' fills my ears and I begin to jump around, thrashing my arms all over the place and shouting the words alongside Olivia's pitch-perfect voice. Quickly, I stop the music and stand still in sudden realisation, analysing myself in the floor-length mirror... am I stimming?

I maintain my gaze towards the mirror and again, play the music, reenacting what I was doing just a moment ago in the swing of my favourite song. I throw my head about, my arms in uncontrollable flaps by my side and my legs throw me up and down in conjunction with my wild hair in time with the beat of the music. I am stimming.

The song concludes and in response my body reluctantly

returns to a static position, craving more, twitching slightly. I stop the playlist and look over the tracks, all of which are those that make me giddy and want to bounce around like Tigger. I rename the playlist: Stim Dancing and look on YouTube for some confirmation that this is actually what I think it is. Confirmation is there, on a video from an autistic woman around my age, who dances in a somewhat similar way to me.

Shock takes over as this sinks in and so many things start to make sense. All the times I went clubbing and lost myself in music and dancing, it was all a form of stimming and that's why I would come away from a night out feeling on top of the world, only to crash down when the hangover kicked in the next day. It all makes sense that I craved tennis every day, the explosive movements were stimming, the weightlifting I do now, it's all stimming.

Now completely distracted from my workout, I type 'forms of stimming' into Google, skip straight to the images and see: *staring off into space, chewing, jumping, biting the inside of the mouth, licking, fidgeting.* I do all of those things and always have done without any knowledge that this was stimming. I think back to my raisin fingers as a child, *that's what that was*, I think laughing to myself about the way I still incessantly lick my fingers whenever I touch dry things. The other kids at swimming used to be so confused about my constant licking and if I didn't lick them my whole body would feel wrong and made me move in strange ways. There were so many clothes I ruined through chewing and sucking them, my mum getting frustrated every time she saw me with my jacket or my hair in my mouth 'you can't be chewing your clothes now, chicken. You have to try be grown up' she would say. I get it, from the external eye it was a strange thing to do, without meaning but to me it was everything I needed to feel safe and okay.

I laugh aloud, thinking of the times I had to fold napkins when I worked in a restaurant. Everyone thought it was the best job because you could sit down and have a chat, but not me, between every fold of a napkin it was be *lick, lick, lick.* Until my mouth was dry, at which point I would get myself a bowl of water and dip my fingers in between each touch of the napkin. My boss would always ask me why the napkins looked like they had water spilt on them, something I never decided to explain to him. I mean how would you even go about explaining that? "Sorry, I have this compulsive need to lick my fingers whenever I touch dry things, if I don't my toes feel all wrong and out of order and I shiver a lot. That's why your napkins are wet, it's only my salvia, no need to worry." There were even times where I would try to use my elbows to press down the crease so that my hands wouldn't have to touch anything. I do not miss that!

Nowadays, I find myself without thought chewing the inside of my mouth, usually when I'm driving and my thoughts are racing, bouncing relentlessly around my head. The chewing, I've now realised is almost constant and I have scar tissue to prove that, that I run my tongue over. Fleetingly, I wonder if my dentist has released and thinks I'm constantly anxious. Now I'm reflecting on it I realise that I suppressed that much stimming behaviour that I physically hurt myself on an almost hourly basis. I wonder, fleetingly if the self-harm I inflicted on myself was part of the stimming behaviour; it's likely it was.

There are so many times that I force myself to sit still in meetings and training and at restaurants when my food is finished. In school, I would wiggle my legs, the book I was holding or chew the tip of my pen, everyone told me to stop but those things were what supported me to listen and stay in my seat. Now, I don't even do those things because they've been conditioned out of me, I sit in discomfort and chew the inside of my mouth or pull away the skin from the outskirts of my nails.

The thoughts begin to escalate and I consider that if I

hadn't been taught to suppress these things perhaps I would do more whole-body stimming like jumping or hand flapping naturally. Maybe I did do those things as a child and never knew. During the interview Dr Hudson had with my parents they said that I would tip toe walk, something that I was never aware of and had no recollection of, which must mean there's other stims I can't remember. I wish I could, and I wish that I would be confident enough to use them in public, but flapping my hands and jumping about around other people doesn't seem appealing right now. As I educate those around me, maybe I'll let them into my secret stims, but for now they're my private things that I will learn to enjoy in solitude.

Abandoning my research, I return to my dancing, happy in the new knowledge of how much it is regulating my body and emotions. After a few more songs, I'm lost in the sound of 'Misery Business' by Paramore, so much so that I don't hear Jack enter the room, laughing at the sight in front of him. Midway through the chorus I turn to see Jack jumping alongside me and remove my headphones, confused.

"What are we doing, my little weirdo?" He smiles, teasingly.

"That was not for your eyes, I'm dancing and enjoying myself, now go away and let me continue." I push him out the room with mock force.

"It was very cute, maybe I'll join in next time." He relents and leaves me in peace. As the door closes and the music restarts a big grin spreads across my face. Maybe I don't have to hide my stimming from everyone.

17
HORRID HENRY & HOOVERS

2004

I like it when mum and dad give me nicknames, especially when they give me tasks. Sometimes, when mum's in a good mood she'll say 'please sweetheart' at the end of the instruction and it makes me feel okay about doing it, a lot of the time I resist whatever she's told me and mould it to be done in my way, which irritates her. When dad puts me to bed at night he calls me a different name for each day of the week, sometimes 'Miglet' or 'chicken' and sometimes even 'my little terrapin' I don't know what a terrapin is but I like to feel special and dad's names for me make me feel just that. I think I fit a terrapin, whatever it might be because I'm a terror quite often at home. A bit ago, I looked in the 'baby names' book mum has and saw that my name was translated as 'terror, ruler of the home' and thought that was about right, I seem to always want things my way at home and this makes my parents stressed a lot. I really try to do things how everyone else wants me to do them but their ways don't work in my brain and I feel more comfortable if I do them in the way I like to.

Mum often tells me that I need to keep Basil on his lead on walks until we're further into the field across the road but I always let him off earlier because otherwise he tugs me and I don't like the feeling of being pulled or attached to something that wants to go a different way to me, just like when mum pulls the shopping trolley. When I get back, mum always asks me if I kept Basil on his lead until we got halfway down the field and I always say "yes" and this makes her angry because she knows I've lied, she can see the field from our kitchen window.

It annoys me that she watches me and I end up storming off. I want to do what mum asks me to do but it always feels so difficult and I don't always want to do whatever adults ask me to do, some of the things they ask are just pointless and make no sense. Mum asks me to dry the washing up after we've eaten tea but it dries overnight on the draining board anyway so why can't we just wait until it's dried the next morning? Mum doesn't like clutter and always wants things tidied away in their exact places and this makes me stressy. I like to have things where they belong too but there's so much pressure to stay tidy and my brain is scatty and I can't keep track of where all my things are and should be and I never see the things that need tidying away.

Sometimes, my parents ask me to do things and my body just doesn't let me do them. I really know I should do what they ask me because it will make everyone happier, me included, but sometimes I just can't. When I'm asked directly it feels like too much demand and my mind and my body says no, even though I will myself to just do it. This happens lots when mum and dad try to teach me new things at sport, I don't like being instructed by people that aren't my coaches and even then it's really difficult to do what they say. Sometimes, mum gives me lots of little things to do all at once and there's too much, too quick and I know she wants it doing there and then but I need it to be in my own time, not anyone else's.

Whenever I'm asked to do something at home, like unpacking the dishwasher, I always get this really hot feeling in my chest and my head goes all cloudy and I try to move my body to do the task but I just can't. I feel sorry for mum when she comes over and gets annoyed at me for not doing what she instructed but that always makes it worse, then I feel even more pressure to do those things and I end up running away. I wish I could be a good daughter, like everyone else who does what their parents ask of them without a massive fight and I do try really hard but I just can't.

Mum often asks me not to do certain things when my friends come over, like not to go in her bedroom or not to get the guinea pigs out of their hutch without her or dad there. Every time, I do whatever she's asked me not to do and I end up getting all sorts of telling off afterwards. Today, Anna came over and we went in mum's bedroom and looked through her jewelry, escaping out the door just as she came back into the house. We giggled to each other and slipped back into my room without her knowing and although I laughed I got this falling feeling in my tummy because I did a bad thing and betrayed mum's trust. For the rest of our playing, I couldn't focus on what Anna was saying and I couldn't think clearly, only thinking of the fact I had done what mum had asked me not to and I wish I could rewind time. I was sure she would find out and of course, she did.

"Why do you do these things when I specifically ask you not to?" Says mum, later on whilst we finish up our dinner at the garden table.

"It's just sometimes I feel like I have this bad thing next to me that tells me to do naughty things and I can't stop myself even though I really don't want to." I respond, looking down at my feet upset with myself.

"What do you mean?"

"Well, you know like people have an angel and a devil on their shoulders? Well, it feels like that and it feels like the little devil tells me to do things."

"Does the devil talk to you?" She asks, quizzically looking towards my dad and then coming down to my level to try and meet my gaze, I turn away.

"Erm sort of, it's like a feeling that I have to do something, and I can't stop myself once it's started and I feel really bad after." Mum strokes my back and says she'll try to help, and I must try to tell her when this happens and try to stop doing things that the devil tells me to do. But there isn't really a devil, and it doesn't tell me in words to do things, it's also not like a devil on my shoulder, I just didn't know how to explain it properly. It's more like this feeling that takes over me, like a fuzz of energy that waits behind me and takes control of my body and mind momentarily and makes me do these things without thinking.

The truth is, it's like I lose my inhibitions in the excitement of seeing my friend and my brain is constantly playing catch up, I just do exactly what I feel like doing in the moment and it's not until after I've finished doing it that I process what I've done and the consequences of it. But mum seems doesn't seem like she's angry with me now that I've told her there's a devil, finally she can see that I'm not doing it on purpose.

Later that night, I hear mum talking to grandma on the phone about her cousin Dawn, who mum said has something called Schizophrenia. Mum explains what I said to her earlier and my grandma listens intently. She asks my grandma questions like: "Did Dawn hear voices?" "how young did it start?" and "do you think I should talk to the doctors?". Grandma must reassure mum because she puts the phone down and sighs in a way that says it's going to be okay.

As well as not doing the things my parents want me to do, when I do try to do things they ask I can't ever seem to do them properly and my parents shout at me lots. Like when they ask me to tidy my room and I never do it exactly how they want it tidied. I just end up organising some of my things and get really distracted by putting my books in alphabetical order that I leave the clothes on the floor, which was the reason I needed to tidy my room. I tell them that they didn't tell me that I specifically needed to put my clothes away but then they think I'm being silly and 'talking back' to them when all I'm trying to do is explain.

Every day, I try really to be a good girl at home, but my brain doesn't seem to work like it does when I'm at school. At school I do exactly as the teachers ask without questions, although I do misunderstand what they mean a lot, but I think they see that I'm trying and let me off. At home, I start doing tasks like making myself a sandwich, but I never tidy away after myself and forget that there's mess. I get stressed when mum tells me to tidy before I eat, because I get hangry, and I just want to eat my sandwich and it's not in the right sequence to tidy up first! At school I don't need to do things like tidying up after myself and even when we do in arts and crafts the teachers give us time warnings and remind us to tidy up, which helps. I think it really frustrates mum and dad that I'm so well-behaved at school but not at home, they can't understand it but I can't explain why either.

A lot of the time, when I'm doing things like unpacking the dishwasher, I get distracted by things on the TV or eating my snack and I forget to unpack the cutlery or the top shelf, mum thinks I'm being lazy or difficult, but I just forget to finish things. Then when she does remind me to finish what I'm doing I shout at her and start to get all hot and want to scream, because it seems that I always get things wrong and need people to point out what I'm not doing. I don't understand why I can't just do what people ask me to do, some days I don't feel like trying because I always know somehow, I'm going to mess it up and make everyone angry.

It's especially difficult when my parents give me really long instructions and I can't remember what they've asked me to do, especially in the morning when my brain doesn't feel like it's warmed up for the day. I always remember the last thing and forget the thing at the start or in the middle and it really frustrates me because I try so hard to hold it in my head. Mum tries to help me remember things by writing me lists of things to do but then I have to decide what to do first and the list feels too big and just reminds me that no one else at school needs a silly task list, just me because I can't get anything right. People tell me I'm just being awkward when I don't do what they ask me, but I just can't remember everything they say and then I get all worried I'll forget, and it gets so much worse.

Today, mummy has asked me to go to the garage for a bin bag and some more food for Basil. I feel cosy and warm in my house and I'm really tired so I don't want to do it, but I slide on my trainers, pushing down the backs and slam the door on my way out. I come back inside and put the dog food on the table, starting to walk back into the living room to sit down and read my 'Harriet the Spy' book.

"Be helpful and make it, I shouldn't have to tell you that, he's your dog," Mum barks. It frustrates me because I don't understand why she didn't tell me 'go and get Basil's food and then make his dinner' instead, so I knew what to expect. I thought I would be going back to read my book, but mum is making me change what I expected and I don't like it. She also didn't say it nicely because she's had a stressful day.

"Fine." I snap and start to make the dog's dinner, he sits patiently whilst I mix his biscuits with horrible smelling goo, some of it gets on my fingers and I want to squeal, the sensation is like being slapped in the face. I start to walk into the living room again to read the book I'm itching to get back to.

"Harry!" Mum's voice raises an octave. "Why have you left it on the side? It needs to go on his mat." How do I not know this? How did I forget to give the dog his dinner when I'd just made it? I start to feel hotter, and I dig my nails into my palms to stop myself hitting something.

"Where's the bin bag you brought in?" She snaps, losing her temper. Oh no, the bin bag I was supposed to get with the dog food, it's still in the garage I forgot about it. She only told me two things to remember, how did I forget one of them? What is wrong with me? I just don't understand. Mum moves towards the front door muttering that if she wants something doing properly, she should just do it herself and then she sees my shoes with their backs bent over from my journey to the garage.

"How many times?" She shouts, picking up one of my trainers and gestures to the ruined back of the shoe. "I have told you until I am blue in the face not to push the backs down on your trainers and to put them on properly. You can't look after anything we get you; you're spoilt!" I hate it when she calls me spoilt, because I'm not, I'm grateful for everything I get but it just feels like too much of a task to look after the things they give me and I just want to make things easier for myself, like bending the backs of my shoes so that I don't have to go and get my flip flops. Sometimes I just go out in my slippers and somehow that's even worse because my parents tell me off for trailing mud into the house.

I can't take it anymore, there's too much to process of all the things I've done incorrectly in a matter of seconds. I feel like I'm the most useless human, I don't need reminding of all the things I haven't finished or the things I've forgotten, it only makes me want to cry. I have tried my hardest all day and I still can't do anything right; I can never be good enough and never what anyone wants. They're all mean, mean, mean and I hate all the adults in the world, they're always telling me to do things and then saying 'no not like that' and everything feels too big and I don't know how to calm down. I just want to read Harriet the Spy and be in quiet and not have mum giving me instruction after instruction. I pick up the trainers and throw them at the front door, screaming in protest. Mum looks shocked but her anger doesn't fade, she just gets redder and redder, her nostrils flaring like they do when she's about to lose her temper.

"I HATE YOU!" I scream, it hurts my throat and tears are burning hot on my face. I can't control my body or anything I'm saying in this moment. I don't want to say I hate mum, but I really, really do right now. I hate everyone and everything.

"You better tidy this up by the time I get back in." She gestures to the bowl of Basil's food that is now scattered across the floor along with my trainers. The door slams behind her, jolting me into focus, I need to get away from this situation, but she'll be even crosser if I don't tidy up. I arrange my trainers back into their place, bending the backs to their original position and bend down to scoop up the biscuits back into the bowl when mum re-enters the house, opening the door onto my arm that's in the way. It's enough to set me off back into my meltdown, I can't cope with the touch that I'm not expecting, and I slam the bowl of biscuits down, causing them to scatter further.

"What are you doing?" She yells.

"Aghhhhhhhhh!" I growl, straining my voice even more, words won't come any more and I attempt an escape from the kitchen to the safety of silence in my bedroom.

"Don't you dare go anywhere, get this tidied up." Mum states, sternly. I can't cope, I need to get away from this, I'm only going to cause more problems if I can't just run away and reset. Mum starts the vacuum and gestures for me to clean up the biscuits with it but the noise of the hoover is too much and as I take control of it I start to cry. This feels too much, it feels painful, it feels unfair and midway through I slam down the hoover and rush upstairs, not understanding what mum is yelling after me as I finally escape.

Reaching my bedroom, I slam the door shut and scuttle to the corner of my bed, leaning against the base and hiding from anyone who might enter. I press my nails hard into the palms and cry uncontrollably, I can barely breathe between the sobs. I can't think, I can't speak, I can't see any way out of this feeling, it's consuming. I know that I need to apologise to mum and tell her how sorry I am that I'm so difficult and I get so wound up so quickly and I can't do whatever she tells me, but those words feel way too difficult. I get a pen and paper and write: *Mummy, I'm so sorry that I'm so awful, I will try harder. Please don't be mad at me, I'm sorry*, then I screw up the piece of paper, there's no point apologising she's still going to be cross, and she always tells me that I shouldn't apologise if I'm going to do the same thing again. I never want to do the same thing again, but I know I will because I'm awful and I can't do as I'm told for my parents, mum especially.

The sound of dad's car reversing up the drive arrives in my ears, and I feel a wave of emotion that he's home from work, which feels a little bit like relief but it's not quite. I like hearing dad arrive home because it signifies it's nearly dinnertime and we can then all sit down and relax for the night with no more demands. The wave of emotion brings a whole new wave of tears that had dried on my cheeks. He enters the house, firmly closing the heavy, front door behind him and immediately I hear mum beginning to retell him the events of the evening and I just know she's just going to give her point of view and nothing about my feelings and thoughts. I get angry again because I know that dad always agrees with her and comes to tell me off when he gets home.

His footsteps start on the stairs, *one, two three* I count the steps, my heart beats faster, I stop crying to listen, *eleven, twelve, thirteen*. I hear him turn into his bedroom and close the door, I don't understand, why is he not coming to say "hello" to me or even come to have a word with me about my behaviour? A few moments later I hear him open and close the bedroom door again and start to descend the stairs, this is not good, this means they're really mad. What do I do now? Do I sit here until they come and get me? Do I go downstairs and apologise? I settle for kicking the floor in rage that will teach them to leave me on my own. I listen, still nothing, I really don't like this feeling. I would rather they tell me how angry they are and tell me I'm the worst child in the world than sit here and be ignored. I rip up the piece of paper with my sorry note, *I'm not sorry I hate them both*.

It's an hour before I realise no one is going to come and speak to me and so I skulk downstairs in need of some confirmation they still love me. I need space and I need to run away when I get overwhelmed, but I can't be on my own for long, it doesn't calm me down, I need help to calm down not be left alone because then I just start hitting myself or digging my nails into my skin and that's painful. Mum and dad are sat in the kitchen, watching the news on the TV like nothing has happened; I spot the hoover and the dog biscuits still scattered on the floor. I know what I have to do but I don't want to do it right now because I don't want to give in, they've ignored me.

No one says anything as I enter the room, they don't even turn to look at me and I shuffle around the corner, sliding onto my seat without a sound. I can't talk, I know they're waiting for me to say sorry, but the words seem like too much to say, they feel like an acceptance of defeat and make me feel too vulnerable. Instead, I write the word 'sorry' again and again on the table with my finger, crying silently when no one sees it or appreciates the gesture. I just want one of them to lean over and put their hand on my hand and let me know everything is okay between us, I don't want to talk, I just want to know it's going to be okay.

"Harry, go and tidy up." Mum says without feeling in her voice, she sounds exhausted, and I know I'm the cause. I slip out of my seat and clean up the remaining biscuits, wincing as the shrill sound of the hoover fills my ears. I finish up and dad gestures for me to sit down, turning off the TV. I guess this means it's time to talk.

"Right, I don't want to keep coming home to this." He gestures at mine and my mum's faces, both blotchy and puffy eyes, it's only then I realise mum has been crying too, I haven't been able to look at anyone's faces until now. I can't stand their gaze on me or the chance of our eyes meeting, it feels too exposing. In that moment I feel like the worst daughter in the world, why am I making my mummy so upset? Why can't I just be a good girl and make everyone I live with happy and not miserable?

We've been arguing for weeks now, almost every night and when dad comes home, we're not speaking but I don't know how to make it better. Mum loses her temper quicker and quicker every time and I just feel like one huge burden. She said she used to be really patient when she was younger and I know that she's not anymore, so that must be my fault. I've made mum easily triggered and unhappy, she must have been happier before she had me.

Dad talks about how I need to start doing things straight away when I'm asked and stop being so 'bloody' difficult. He says I need to start thinking about how to help at home and stop being so defiant; I need to stop being angry when I'm reminded of things that I forget. It's all things that I need to change and not anybody else, which tells me my thoughts about it all being my fault were right. I want to ask them to consider asking me to do things in nicer ways or clearly, so I know what to expect but I daren't, I just want to stop them being angry with me right now. That's the most important thing, everyone else must be happy and then I will be happy too.

I agree to it all, but I know that I will only do it again; I don't know how to make myself better at these things because I just keep trying and trying and nothing ever works. There are so many times I've thought about running away with Scruffy in my bag and Basil on a lead. I would go down to the woods where we do our dog walks and sit between the trees, quietly undisturbed. If I ran away would mum and dad feel bad and stop giving me so many things to do? Would they stop seeing me as such a pain? I never quite get around to leaving though, sometimes I pack the bag, but I can't make it out of the front door.

I look down at the table the entire time my parents are speaking, unable to speak or look at anyone. I wish they would stop looking at me; I don't want to be looked at. I hide from them as much as I can, scrunching my hands over my face and pressing until I feel pressure in my eyes. It's better than having to look at anyone and this way I can't tell if anyone is looking at me, I can just hear their voices. I zone out of what they're saying for a while and think about the TV programmes I watch sometimes: Dennis the Menice and The Tasmanian Devil, I can see how alike they are to me. Dennis is always being so awful to everyone, and the Tasmanian Devil is just a whirlwind of mess and annoyance. Maybe they should make a cartoon of me 'Horrid Harry', I think about mentioning the idea to my parents but suddenly, I feel mummy press her hands on either side of my face.

"I love you so much, sweetheart." She says a wobble in her voice. This makes me cry, everything I do wrong, and she still loves me. I feel terrible that I can't use words to say it back, but I just can't. I cuddle with mum all evening and when we go to bed, I pass her a little note to say that I'm sorry under her bedroom door. I hope she reads it and smiles and knows how much I love her back. I need to try to be better for my wonderful mum; I can be good all day at school and do everything that I'm asked so I must be able to do it at home.

My mum deserves to be happy because she's the very best. She helps me with so many things and plays sports with me way past anyone else will because they all get bored. She makes me my favourite foods and lets me have extra cheese on everything even when it means she gets less. At the end of every school day, she wants to know everything that I did and will listen to me talk about all the things that have upset me with the other children at school. She holds my hand whenever we go somewhere new and speaks for me when I can't speak myself. I love her the most in the world and I know she loves me just like that too. I'm very lucky so I need to try to make her as happy as she makes me.

18
POWER POSES & PRESENTATIONS

March 2022

It's been three weeks since I opened up to people about my diagnosis and today, I am delivering a talk called: *Hat Talks: Being diagnosed as Autistic at Twenty-Six*. Jenny, a Speech and Language Therapist who I went to university with contacted me to do a presentation for the charity she works for, and I just couldn't refuse the opportunity to make more people aware of autism. I'm absolutely bricking it and it's been all I've been thinking about ever since she asked me, I've hyperfocused into the early hours of a couple of mornings in the last three weeks, thinking of things to add into my talk. I want to get everything I need to say into twenty minutes but I'm aware that's never going to happen. Instead, I opt for a punchy and emotional speech that hopefully will evoke a lot of thought from everyone.

With five minutes until the presentation, I practice my power poses, put on a comfortable jumper and stroke Meeno so that the nerves will calm. The talk is on Teams, as I log on I see Jenny's friendly face along with lots of unfamiliar people, my feet find Meeno under the desk so that I feel comforted.

"Hello everyone and welcome to our final presentation of our neurodiversity celebration week!" Jenny introduces the talk and me and I share my screen with a PowerPoint presentation dad has helped me to create.

"Hello everyone, it's wonderful to be here today talking to you all about autism." I start, video turned off so that I don't distract myself. I start the presentation with an introduction to myself, with and without my identity and run through my childhood years, including food aversions, 'shyness' and Selective Mutism. I can see Jenny smiling on the screen as I start to talk about the university days and how I made none of my lecturers and was overshadowed by mental health difficulties, it all makes sense to her now because she was there. Now, onto the hard-hitting stuff, I take a deep breath and dive into the parts of the talk that made me emotional every time I practiced it.

"As a result of being diagnosed later in life, I have lived 26 years feeling shame that I couldn't be what other people needed from me, worrying over every stumble in my social interactions and experiencing depression and anxiety because the world is just too much at times.

"When I told family and close friends about my diagnosis I think it was a bit of a shock to people, they didn't see me as being autistic, because I didn't look autistic to them. They knew the masked version of me and how the world had changed me to look more neurotypical, but really underneath that that isn't who I am. For a period of time, I worried that if I told people they would have a different view of me and maybe wouldn't like me anymore. I worried that people would change around me and talk differently to me and focus on the fact that I was Autistic. So, when I told people, I was shocked when I realised I wasn't scared of them changing towards me at all, I was scared that they *wouldn't* change towards me. I've struggled with the fact that people haven't asked how to support me, and my communication needs because they think I'm a mild version of autism and I don't really need support.

"I learnt that I couldn't make my own decisions because everyone told me that what I was choosing wasn't right, they told me I'd made the 'wrong' choice, then it's not really a choice is it? I relied on my parents to help me choose clothes because people told me I wore the wrong things. Every single decision I made I passed through other people. I want this to stop happening to neurodivergent people, because other people think they know what's right or what's best for us and they don't. It's so important that my voice and every other autistic person's voice are listened to for what they are really saying.

"I've always been told that I spoke too little, then too much and sometimes over the top of people so I was rude. I was told that I dominated conversations and spoke about myself too much. I've been judged for the way I eat, too much, too little, in a strange way like nibbling or eating the edges of something first. I've been told not to talk about something that interests me too much because it can get boring for other people. I'm too this, too that, I could never just be me!" Jenny's reaction to this is just what I wanted from the audience, she's clearly emotional. I end the talk with something Jack helped me put together.

"The last thing I would like to say for people who feel a bit different or struggle to use words. Being different is never less, you are wonderful just as you are, being completely you is an incredible thing and it would be oh so boring if everyone were all the same!" Jenny and the other audience members enter the screen again as I stop sharing my presentation.

"Gosh, that was so emotional, maybe that's because I know Harry. Thank you so much, that was incredible. I would like to open the floor to any questions in the last few minutes we have." Jenny requests and people thank me for my presentation, describing it as very eye-opening and inspirational.

"I think it would be really important to ask you, I'm sure in our work place we have autistic employees and I would really like to know what you would suggest for us to better support those people." Another person asks.

"Wow, that's a question." I laugh, "There are so many things, but I think the first thing that springs to mind is to never assume. So, a lot of people see me as doing really well, you know I've got a car, a house, a good career, they see me turn up to work and think 'yeah you're smashing life, you don't need support', when in reality I can come home after a day of work to complete shutdown, be mute for hours and unable to perform basic tasks. I don't want to get into high and low functioning levels, but I would say to never presume someone's circumstances and how their disability affects them."

"I think that's a great one to finish on, Harry." Announces Jenny, "Thank you again so much for speaking to us all today, it's been fantastic and I can see there's a lot of people in the comments throughout giving claps and love heart reactions." I end the call and take a big, deep breath, without doubt that is the best experience I've ever had. I know in this moment that this is what I want to do, I want to do talks and advocate for autistic people as much as I can. I want to be a voice that gets listen to and evokes some change. No matter how small that step is today, it feels like it's my greatest achievement to date, even my graduation cannot compare. I have found my purpose.

*   *   *

Two weeks later, my grandparents and parents gather around the TV screen to listen to and watch the recorded presentation. They all watch in silence and at one point I catch mum's eyes glisten with tears, she dabs secretly away at them, not letting on to anyone that she's emotional. The video draws to an end and my grandma turns to me.

"Wow, we have no idea what you've been through have we?" She studies my face; I wonder if she's really seeing me for the first time. Does she understand me now? Mum talks to her about all the parenting advice my grandparents gave to her and how none of it worked because of me being autistic.

"Grandma, I wasn't being difficult by not eating the

food I was given. I literally saw it and immediately started to retch; it was my sensory aversions nothing to do with choice."

"I see that now." She smiles at me, one of her warm and understanding smiles. She turns to my mum and gives her the same smile, which is just what I needed. The reason I showed my grandparents the presentation was that they would finally understand why my mum parented me in the way that she did. I hoped that they would find acceptance of the things she did that differed from what they advised, and it seems that's happened today. Dad places a hand on my shoulder and whispers.

"Proud of you chicken." It's all he needs to say, he's been listening to extracts of my book and the presentation for a while now, he knows the weight of this stuff. I catch my mum looking at me in a new way, each time she thinks I don't see it but I do and I know that mum will speak to me later when everyone else has gone. It's not her style to talk about emotions when other people are around. Later, as I put on my coat to leave, she envelops me in a hug.

"I got really emotional earlier." She says into my ear, "We've had some experiences, haven't we?" Those words are all I need, mum and I have been through the wars together, we've felt each other's emotions throughout it all and there are no words that would ever begin to describe the experience. We've both had too many times of seeing each other cry and breaking down in front of each other, struggling to cope with the seriousness of my fragile state of mind. Our bond is something outside of the realms of mother and daughter, the words to explain it don't feature in the dictionary and even if they did, they wouldn't do it justice.

19
AN ONSTAGE ACCIDENT

2005

Christina is center stage, loudly announcing her lines to the empty village hall. Maisie and I stand further back on the stage, nervously waiting for our turn to deliver our lines and practice before the big night next week. Every year, we put on a school production at Christmas and this year Maisie, and I have a bigger part because we're in year five now, next year it will be us doing the big parts in the play. I love the play; I'm good at acting because I do it all day, every day anyway. I'm always pretending to be someone else, a character I love in a book or from my own made-up stories.

Recently, I've been Katie, the cool girl who everyone likes and wants to be friends with, she's ultra-confident and doesn't let the year sixes say mean things to her or punch her in the stomach. I'm practicing being Katie because next year I'll be one of the oldest in the school and I won't need to worry about people being mean to me anymore or making fun of the things I say in class. Most of the kids who are younger than me at school like me so it's only seven months to go before all the year sixes leave and I'm popular at school.

Last week, all the year sixes went on a school trip to prepare them for senior school, and it was the best day ever. I got to play in the big playground without worrying about what everyone thought of me, and I didn't get called a baby once for playing made up games with Ben and Peter.

But for now, year six are very much head of the school and I'm reminded of that by how long Christina's speech is going on for. I'm not worried about my lines right now; I'm only focused on the fact that I really, *really* need the toilet and all the teachers are preoccupied by Christina's rubbish acting. I shuffle from one foot to the next, crossing and uncrossing my legs, holding my fists really tight and humming under my breath. Maisie buries her elbow into my side and puts her finger to her mouth in a gesture that tells me to shut up.

Christina finishes her lines but then it's straight into Greg's lines and I've missed my chance to exit the stage. I frantically look around for a teacher to signal my distress to but they're all busy organising costumes or rehearsing lines with everyone else. I don't know what to do, mum has said that if I need the toilet I need to ask someone, but I've also just been told by the teachers that we must not interrupt each other's lines. Plus, I always get told off for interrupting other people when they talk, and the year sixes give me evil eyes when I do this and I'm trying to be Katie and Katie is cool and doesn't annoy people. So instead, I'm just going to be quiet and wait until I'm called to move off the stage. I bite my lip and start to chew the inside of my mouth to distract myself from the need to wee. This happens very often because I never know that I need to use the toilet until the very last minute and then sometimes it's just too late.

Last year, grandma and grandpa took me to Blackpool to go and see Aunty Joan, I'm not really sure how we're related but I know that she's nice and I really like going to her house because grandpa always takes me to the massive toy shop on the way home and I get to pick a toy that I really want, last time I got some new clothes for My Scenes. No one seems to understand why I like the clothes the most, I just like to dress them up how I would like to look but can never look because those clothes would be uncomfortable and too girly for me.

I always stay in the same room as my grandparents when we go away, and they blow up an air mattress next to their bed for me. This is okay because I can sleep anywhere, it doesn't have to be comfy, I fall asleep really quick because I'm always really tired on a night. While we were away, I weed on the air mattress a few times because they told me not to get up in the night and wake them up so I just tried to go back to sleep when I woke needing the toilet. I also didn't really know the house and I felt scared to get up in the dark and find the toilet, because that's when bad things happen, in the middle of the night. They were really angry with me and told me I was too old to be weeing the bed and called mum to tell her and ask her why I might do that. Mum said she didn't know; I don't understand why they didn't just ask me.

I worry whenever we go somewhere new, because I don't know where the toilets are. I especially don't like it when it's just me and dad and I have to go into the toilet by myself. When we went on a cruise ship with grandma and grandpa, dad took me to the men's toilets and told me not to lock the door, but when I got in there, I had to lock the door because mum always says I should never leave the door open to the toilet in public, even though we do that at home. All these rules are so very confusing. So, I locked the door and once I'd finished I couldn't open it again and I sat on the floor rocking back and forth unable to ask anyone to help me, until eventually dad came in to find me and I couldn't speak I could only wave my hand out the bottom of the cubicle.

Dad asked me if I could squeeze out and I tried but the gap was tiny and only Jess, my teddy could fit. Dad took Jess and told me that he would go and get someone to help, I cried because I was scared he was going to leave me forever and I didn't want to be left trapped behind the door unable to speak. I also didn't like speaking to people through a door because I couldn't see their face to understand what they were saying. I didn't like it that dad's voice was there, but I couldn't see him, it just made me more distressed.

The next thing I heard was an announcement on the speakers outside of the toilets and the captain was asked to come and assist in the male toilets on the top deck. Dad came in with a man whose voice was very deep and I didn't like hearing his voice without his face, he sounded like a big, grizzly bear.

"Okay, let's get you out of there, sweetheart." The gruff voice said through the door, "Can you try to pull the lock for me?" I couldn't reply with my voice and dad told the captain this.

"Just show me with your hand if you can do it." Says dad, my hand protruded out the bottom with a thumbs down. The captain tried to ram the door open with his shoulder, telling me to stay back but it didn't budge, it was all very frightening. He tried to squeeze over the top of the cubicle, so I saw his face and immediately felt better because he looked very friendly and had a hairy face like a teddy bear.

The captain decided after much squeezing and sighing we needed someone else, so he made an announcement on the speakers asking for the 'skinniest', male crew member on board. Within a few minutes I heard another male voice say, "okay I'm coming over" which I did not like. I did not want a scary voiced, probably very hairy and tall man in my cubicle. This was my cubicle. It's the worst sharing my swimming changing cubicle with another girl at school; it makes me feel like a banana, all peeled and squished. The new man's hairy head appeared over the top of the cubicle and half his beanstalk-like body and reached his arms down into the toilet for me to grab on to. I didn't like the thought of being grabbed by someone I didn't know, especially a man who was smiling at me in a distressing situation, but I also didn't like the thought of being trapped in her forever, so I allowed him to pull me out into safety.

Mum always checks now if I need to wee before we go or leave anywhere because she knows that I won't tell her. She even makes me go to the toilet before we go somewhere but I say don't need it, it turns out most of the time I do need to go but my body hasn't told me yet. Mum tells me that I should always make sure I make the toilet part of my routine when we go on school trips because I don't want to embarrass myself when I'm with my friends.

Other people are really funny about the toilet, and they get all weirded out if you tell them you need a wee or a poo. My family always talk about which one we are going for because then we know how long we are going to be before we come back. Last time I asked Mrs Burns if I could go for a poo, she told me that yes, I could but next time I could just ask to go to the toilet, she didn't need to know why I was going. I thought she might have appreciated the heads up if I was a bit longer than usual.

Christina starts her lines again and I just can't hold it any longer, wee sneaks its way out of my bladder and my knickers and tights become soaked, as I stare at the puddle below me. Maisie gaps and steps aside, shocked.

"Miss, miss!" She yells and everyone on the stage turns to look.

"Oh goodness," says Mrs Howell as she ushers me off stage. "What happened?" She asks when we get off the stage and into the toilet. I'm glad we've stopped walking; I didn't like the feel of my feet squelching in my shoes. I don't speak, thinking about the repercussions of what has just happened. I will never be Katie as much as I try I always end up doing the wrong thing. They said not to interrupt; I don't understand what I was supposed to do. I think of Anna and how this would never happen to her, she always knows the right thing to do and if she was next to me, I'd have been able to ask her for help and the right thing to do. If I had a friend who really understood me at school, then maybe these silly things wouldn't keep happening to me.

"Were you nervous about your lines?" Asks Mrs Howell, bewildered. I shake my head and look down at the floor to the pile of wet clothes she's asked me to remove. She hands me a towel and some clean clothes from the costumes, signaling for me to put them on, it feels all wrong I have no knickers on, and you can't not wear knickers at school. I tried that once and got told off.

"Why did you not just ask?" She comes down to my level, hoping to catch my eyes but instead I turn my face away.

"You told everyone not to interrupt other peoples' lines." I mutter.

"Yes, but you could have just left the stage or put your hand up." She looks at me quizzically. It should be me looking confused, what she's saying is silly, she told me not to interrupt and that includes leaving the stage or putting my hand up, does it not? They've told me off for putting my hand up on stage before and I was told to put it down. Adults are so confusing with their weird rules and instructions. I am beckoned to return to the stage in my original position, the puddle is gone, and everyone stares at me in disgust as I assume my place on the stage. Maisie stands further away from me as Christina redoes her scene.

*   *   *

After rehearsals, mum comes to pick me up from the village hall and I don't meet her eye as she enters, knowing I've embarrassed her. Mrs Howell has told me to wait back so she can speak to mum before we leave. She relays the details of the puddle incident to mum and when I glance fleetingly at her face, she looks concerned.

"She's done this before." Says mum, "I don't

understand why she won't just ask you; she knows she can put her hand up if she needs the toilet, I've told her she can do that in class." *But this isn't class*, I think, *the rules are different here.*

"I don't know but she didn't even try to make us aware." Mrs Howell continues, and I zone out of the conversation, they're talking about me not with me. I understand everything they are saying, even if they whisper it, it still means the same. When they're done, mum gives me a hug and takes a clear bag of clothes from Mrs Howell that has my puddle outfit in. Only, my tights are still on the radiator by the side of the stage, and it feels like too much effort to use my voice to tell mum we'd forgotten them.

20
WITHOUT WORDS, I'M STILL HEARD

April 2022

A few nights ago, Jack had asked me to go and pick him some euros up from Tesco for his holiday to Portugal. I was supposed to do it yesterday but just couldn't work myself up to it, spending all day in bed; the first day I'd done this since my university days. I'd woken at twelve and taken Meeno for a walk in my pyjamas before crawling back to my bed, not eating until Jack got home at five.

This morning, I wake still exhausted, it's the first day of the Easter holidays but I've been exhausted for so long that I'd already predicted this week would be full of sleep, isolation and burying my head in the fantasy world of books. It's normal for me to spend the first week of my school holidays like this, recovering from the onslaught of the school term. I can feel in my body that today is going to be a no words day and all the small tasks I have to complete today suddenly feel way too big. I roll over to my side and I'm immediately greeted by a wet nose on my head, it seems Meeno has snuck his way onto my pillow and is once again sleeping on my head. I smile at him and pull him down to my chest for his favourite part of the day - a morning cuddle. The appreciation I have for this little creature this morning is unparalleled; he allows silence without demand, indicating his needs through pawing at me instead of words that would feel too horrendous to hear this morning.

I catch sight of Jack's packed suitcase in the corner of the bedroom and sigh internally, apparently any kind of voice is not happening today. My chest feels tight as I think about being left in the house by myself for days on end, in a low mood and fragile state of mind, without anyone to support me. I have to remind myself that today is not five years ago, now I can be by myself without chaos, destruction and unpredictable impulses. Still the tightness in my chest doesn't leave and I worry about communicating with people when I don't have anyone to rely on, should this period of voicelessness continue. I consider texting my parents and asking to stay at their house for a couple of nights, but I quickly dismiss the thought as panic rises of an expectation to speak, keep things tidy and a change to my routine.

I spend the whole morning swapping from room to room, trying to find inspiration to exercise, go to the gym and eventually to Tesco, when my voice returns. The task of preparing to go out and walk Meeno feels overwhelming, and I delay it for as long as I can. At one o'clock, he leaps onto the sofa next to me and places his paws on my chest, leaning his head towards me to lick my face, as I push his mouth away he leaps away and runs to the front door, he's desperate for some stimulation. It takes maximum effort to organise the things I need, I'm unaware of where any of the things I need are: walking boots, lead, harness, poo bags, a tissue, headphones, a cap, and appropriate clothes. It takes me twenty minutes just to gather the items, frequently going in and out of rooms having forgotten yet another thing I've missed from the list, whilst collecting another. I can feel frustration rising in me, choking me and I fight back tears. Why does it have to be this hard some days? Why does my brain betray me like this?

I'm thankful for Meeno on days like today; having fresh air, feeling some sun on my face and space to clear my thoughts makes me feel a little better. I always feel better when I've achieved something in my day and a walk feels like a massive achievement today. Still, it gets to four and I still haven't been to Tesco, Jack needs to leave for the airport at five-thirty. I know I have to do this now, with or without voice. I've been trying to stop myself from forcing speech for weeks now; maybe this is my opportunity to finally make that first, brave step.

All of my life I've been told to speak, to speak louder, use politeness markers, full sentences, a more approachable tone, welcoming facial expression alongside my speech. I've been told I must use voice to be valuable and heard. Having heard this for twenty-six years this is not an easy pattern to break, even when I support my students to self-advocate for communication alternatives. I feel like a fraud, how can I expect them to feel worthy when using Alternative and Augmentative Communication (AAC) whilst I don't? Today is the day, I'm going to push past all of this internalised ableism and do what is good for me. For the first time in weeks, I feel a spike of positive emotion, this feels right.

The next ten minutes is spent writing what I might want and need to say on pieces of paper. I'm nervous but I'm excited. Meeno picks up a piece of paper which reads 'thank you' and holds it in his mouth, sitting with a cheeky posture next to the sofa. I snap a picture of him with it in his mouth; I'm going to want to remember this first act of courage.

On the drive to Tesco, I ruminate over the potential negative response to my communication. I worry that I'll get to the counter and opt out, forcing voice instead. I'm so nervous that when I get up to the counter, I press the piece of paper with my communication up to the cashier's window with a bang. She looks taken aback and looks from me to the piece of paper, before warmly smiling and confirming that I want an assortment of five, ten and twenty notes. She scrunches her eyes at the note when reading again and so I push it under the window for her and she smiles, thanking me.

The pressure mounts as she organises the notes from the bank, is she going to ask me a question I can't answer with yes or no or one of my pre-written notes? Is she going to look at me funny and wonder why I'm not speaking? Is she going to ask me why I'm not speaking or make an ableist assumption? I realise I'm pressing my thumbs into my fists, a sign that I'm experiencing ridiculous anxiety. She does none of the things I expect and slides the notes under the window whilst smiling at me and thanking me for my custom.

I suddenly relax, what I thought would be a horrendous experience has actually been a positive one and everything that I'd hoped for, I feel comfortable in this exchange and finally meet her eye. Instead of pulling out the pre-written note from my purse, I press my palm to my chin and push my hand downwards in the sign for 'thank you' whilst mouthing the words. She smiles as I leave and as I walk away it feels like I've just experienced the biggest achievement of my life. This is something I can do again and again; I've been courageous and used communication that's right for me and not everyone else. I immediately post the picture of Meeno to my Hat Talks Instagram page along with the caption:

Today was my first use of AAC (alternative communication) in the community. This took a lot of courage and I'm so proud of myself. Meeno helped as you can see. I've been completely mute today and usually I would force myself into speech at the detriment of my mental health. But not today, today I kicked ableism's butt and did what suited MY communication needs not everyone else's.

For weeks I've been trying to find the courage to start using alternative communication when I go to shops but have always backed out last minute, worried about people's reactions. My issue is that I've been told all my life to force myself to speak otherwise I'm being 'childish', 'rude' or 'hard work'. That's created so much internal ableism, where I've told myself that if I can force myself into speech then I should, regardless of the consequences because otherwise I'm being high maintenance.

Speech is no more valuable than any other communication. My voice deserves to be heard no matter which way I use it. And that goes for everyone else! I'm an AAC using Speech & Language Therapist and proud.

When Jack returns from work, my voice has returned and I use it to wish him a wonderful trip and tell him I'll miss him. If I had used my voice in Tesco earlier, those words would never have been exchanged.

21
LUCY'S SILLY APPLES & A GIANT GIRL

2007

Maths has always been okay at school, but this year it's really hard. My Maths teacher doesn't explain things very clearly and we move onto the next thing without me being sure of the last. I don't like Maths anymore and I don't like her name – Mrs Bainbridge, there's too many bs and ds and I can't write her name without putting them the wrong way around. Maths books are red and there's lots of red pen in mine but not in Ben and Peter's, she likes them both because they understand what she is teaching them but I'm just a bit lost and she doesn't like me.

We learn Maths in a different room from year five,

downstairs in my old year four classroom, where Mrs Smith taught us and my least favourite year, she was scary and looked like an evil koala. She told me off for colouring in the wrong way and always knew by the patterns of my colouring that I had not turned the page round to colour in nice, straight lines. I don't have good memories of this classroom and so I don't like being in here. Mrs Bainbridge always uses a blackboard that's low down on the wall, and I don't like the feel of the chalk beneath my fingers when she asks me to come up and solve the problem. She won't even let me wipe the chalk off my fingers when I've finished, and I can't wipe them on my clothes either so I just have to lick them whenever she turns around.

A lot of the time in Maths, I look out of the window at the younger kids playing in the playground and Mrs Bainbridge smacks her hand down on the table to get my attention, which is loud and scary. She tells me that I maybe if I paid attention like the rest of my class then maybe I wouldn't be so far behind. I don't like being behind everyone else, I'm used to being the cleverest in the class and I get all panicked and hot when I am not.

Mrs Bainbridge calls mum and dad into school for a meeting about my slow progress one night after school. They were surprised when she told them because I've always been really clever at school and Maths has never been a problem before.

"The penny is just not dropping." She announces, I don't really know what penny she is referring to but then she explains that I can't do mental Maths quickly enough and I just keep making silly mistakes in my work. She's started doing year seven Maths to prepare us for senior school and I'm just not getting it because I can't apply what I've learnt in year six to these new sums. I don't really understand what she's on about, all of the questions that she's giving us are new, they're all written down in weird sentences that ask you to work out a Maths sum but they're really unclear of what the sum is. Mrs Bainbridge gives mum and dad an example.

"Lucy has 154 apples, which she needs to divide between three people, how many apples are remaining? Can you work this out for me Harry?" I write down 154 divided by 3 and tell her the outcome.

"You see what I mean?" She turns to my parents, "she's not reading the question. What it is asking for, is not how many apples each person has, it's how many are left over at the end." I don't understand this; the question is confusing, why can't the question just tell me exactly what it wants me to do and not some weird code that I have to figure out that everyone else just seems to get.

"I'm really concerned about her progress when she gets to year seven, if she is not able to get this now, she will get left behind." She continues. My parents tell me not to worry on the car ride home and ask me if I would like them to get me a Maths tutor. And yes, I think I would.

*   *   *

My Maths tutor arrives at our house the following week, she turns up with a briefcase and some low-rimmed glasses. Mum offers her a cup of tea and a warm welcome; I however stay silent, managing a mumbled "hello". I find it difficult having new people in my home and I would much prefer it if mum stayed in the kitchen with us to support the conversation, but she doesn't, instead going to clean the house. I stare after her as the door closes firmly behind her.

"So, tell me about your favourite things." She starts. I feel confused; I thought she was here to help me with Maths? I hate small talk; it makes me squirm and I never know what to say and when we should start talking about the actual topic we are here to discuss.

"Erm, English, tennis, writing stories, my dog and spaghetti bolognaise." I stutter, put off by the unexpected question. I search her face for confirmation that this was the right answer.

"Interesting, Maths isn't on the list." She smiles, have I failed the test? "Let's change that, shall we?" Over the next few weeks, my tutor asks me Maths questions about portions of spaghetti bolognaise and tennis balls and books. She breaks down the questions into visuals, showing me what each style of question is asking for. We come across Lucy and her silly apples, and she shows me what the question means by underlining all of the important information and guiding me through how to do it without expecting me to do it myself.

After four weeks, she sits my mum down and tells her that she doesn't know what that silly Maths teacher, Mrs Painbridge was on about, and Harry is going to be a great Mathematician. I laugh, because Mrs Bainbridge *is* a pain. I don't want to do anything with Maths, but I like that she says that, she understood what I needed to understand the task and helped me, not tested me.

*   *   *

When I take my year six tests a few weeks later I ace every single one, including Maths and think about shoving my 80% score in Mrs Painbridge's face. Mum treats me to a chocolate fudge cake for achieving above 75% in every test and tells me that I've got myself into the schools on my chosen list. Mum and dad are very happy and so is grandpa but all I can think about is the imminent doom of senior school. I don't like change and all I've ever known is Sunflowers, I really don't want to go to school anywhere else, especially one that's bigger.

Mum organises some tours around different schools in our area and further afield. In our final parents' evening, all of the teachers tell my parents that a small school would be better for me just because I'm so shy and take a long time to volunteer and get involved in class. Mum worries that my local high schools will be too big for me, and I will get overwhelmed and bullied, I don't really understand why I'd get bullied but the thought of a big school scares me anyway, so I agree.

A few years ago, my parents booked me in for an operation on my ears because they stuck out really badly; some of the kids of the playground had started calling me names like Dumbo. My mum took me to a specialist in ears and asked him if he thought I would be eligible for my ears pinning back, which he agreed, "yes definitely". When they pinned my ears back, all they did was take the hard stuff out the back of my ear and stitched it to my head, so my ears don't really move off my head now and I have scars at the back of my ears. For a while, I had to wear a white bandage around my head and ears whilst they healed, and it was really uncomfortable to sleep on them. I liked the bandage, because people gave me a bit more space and seemed to be nicer to me and didn't tell me off as much. People always had something to talk to me about and they gave me lots of attention. I also didn't have to worry as much about loud sounds because the bandage muffled them.

I was a bit sad when they took the bandage off and everything went back to normal, because everyone was really short with me again and didn't give me the space I wanted. Mum says that my ears got pinned back because I looked a bit different, and it might mean that kids would be nasty to me when I got to senior school. I feel different from people anyway and they always tease me for being a bit weird, so I guess having my ears fixed makes me appear a bit more normal, at least on the surface.

The first school we look around is Hogsworth Grammar, it's where two of the kids from Sunflowers went to, Peter and Daisy. We arrive at the school, its driveway coated in greenery and thick woodland, as we get out of the car a bus full of children arrives and they all pile out with their grey, blue and red uniform and matching hats. I love hats but I do *not* like those hats, the ones that snap around your neck on an elastic band. I hate those hats because they just make my neck feel squished and when people ping them it gives me all sorts of scared feelings.

A tour guide for the school, Mrs Brown, walks us around and as we enter each classroom the children stand up to greet us and say "hello Mrs Brown" followed by stares at the new girl. I hate this situation, it's all wrong and I hide behind my mum; the more Mrs Brown tries to speak to me the more I stay silent and hide from her.

"She's very shy." My mum laughs nervously, trying to push me further forwards, my arm resists.

"It's okay, I guess that's what small class sizes are good for." She responds and starts chattering to my parents about how comfortable I would feel in the size classes they have. I don't think I'd like being at this school *at all* the corridors make me feel all squished and everything feels all on top of everything and all the kids look strange in their silly uniforms. I don't want to be one of them. Mrs Brown leads us to the final classroom we will be seeing today.

"This is our year six, so the class you would be moving up to secondary school with." She smiles at me; I gulp this feels too much pressure. I want to make a good impression on my new peers, and I don't feel ready to meet them, I want to do this when I've got myself into my mask and I feel more confident and then maybe they'll like me. They won't like me if I'm quiet Harry, hidden behind her mummy. They'll all think that Harry is a baby; I need them to see the cool Harry.

The door swings open and I meet eyes with Peter straight away, he gives me a big grin and I feel safe all of a sudden, I know someone. But then they all stand up and a giant girl looks down at me with evil eyes and that's it I'm back to quiet Harry, hiding from view. Sometimes when I first see people, I automatically know they don't like the look of me because their face says so and I am always right and I know that the giant girl does not like me and if she's that big then she would punch me so much harder than any of the kids at Sunflowers ever would. I've made my decision; I am not going to school with giant girl.

Westgate Girls is next, and I know before we even set off for the school that it is not the place for me, an all-girls' school, girls don't usually like me. The school feels like a prison, all red brick and high up, it feels suffocating. The head girl and a teacher greet us and I know the girl isn't all she seems to be, little Miss Perfect with her braids and fake smile, she doesn't want to show me round the school any more than I want to be here. I've never been in one place with so many girls and it's nauseating, I long for Peter and Ben, probably on the playground now, making up games without me. As soon as we leave the school mum knows I've been uncomfortable the entire time.

"I know you're not keen, but it's a really good school and they're offering you a scholarship, I think you should try the taster day, it will be good for you." She smiles and I want to scream at her, this is *not* a place for me, and she should know that.

The last school we visit is Southly, the one I felt most optimistic about because this is where Linda and Will moved to last year and they seem to really like it. The brochure seemed friendly too. We approach the school on a sunny day, it's so quiet and serene and lost in the countryside of Wakefield, not in the center like Westgate Girls. Climbing out of the car, there's a long walk to the front gates and I welcome this, being able to walk a bit before I enter a building always helps so I can give myself time to think about what I'm going to say and picture what the interior will be like.

As we enter the gates, it overwhelms me how open the school is; there's a modern building over on the left, a really old building and the headmaster's house on the right and straight ahead is a grand building, where students are filtering in for assembly. Everything feels light and airy and there's trees planted with spaces of lawn all across the school, including a lawn tennis court. A chirpy girl and an old, lady teacher welcome us into the school and start talking about all of the resources they have to my parents, I'm not listening, instead taking in the environment and the silence of the halls. Now and again, I hear the occasional word, which spikes my interest 'tennis courts', 'swimming pool', 'acres of land for athletics' and 'English department'. They show us the pool attached to the school and the eight tennis courts, squash court and fields attached for rugby and hockey and cricket.

"We're very sports focused here." Smiles the P.E. teacher we've just been introduced to.

"Well Harry is an excellent tennis player and can really take a hand to any sport you throw at her." My mum declares, placing her hand on my back. We end the tour in the chapel, attached to school and I enjoy staring at the stained-glass windows whilst the adults talk about opportunities. There's a stillness about the school, even when the students are out of classes, it never seems too boisterous or loud and everyone seems to be smiling and friendly, saying 'hello' whenever we pass.

Westgate Girls felt unfriendly, and everyone looked you up and down like competition, here everyone just wanted to acknowledge you as they passed you by, they welcomed you to be part of the team. *I think I like it here.* Mum and dad thank our tour guides and I smile with gratitude, dad slides his arm around my shoulders, guiding me back through the big black gates on the way to our car. Before we leave the blissful feeling, I turn around once more to take in the school that I know I'll be happy in in September.

*   *   *

"Mum, I really don't want to go." I hide my face, pressing my fingers into my eyes like I do when I really want to shut everything out and the scary feelings come.

"You promised me you would try it, and I said that if you didn't like it then you never have to go back again." Mum pleads with me, "But we have to get the right school and that means you have to think about other ones too." Mum is talking about Westgate Girls, I promised her I would go for the taster session just to rule it out before making my decision. I know I won't change my mind, that school is hell, only without boys. I tried to put on my girliest outfit this morning to ensure I fit in, but even that was jeans and a slightly peach top, mum braided my hair like some of the other girls I saw at the school, two little braids right at the front, it's annoying having the hair on my face but I need to fit in.

Mum drops me off and gives me a big kiss, reassuring me that everyone is in the same boat today and no one knows anyone else so it will be fun. I know more than one person, Grace and Maisie and I don't like it when they're both together because then they're mean to me. We're divided into three different groups when we arrive and I know no one in my group, I tag onto a girl who seems to be on her own too and we form a bond by shyly greeting each other with a smile and awkwardly standing next to each other, away from everyone else. I don't think she wants to come to this school either.

The whole experience is painful, and I feel on edge the whole time, worrying about what silly thing I might say next, so I just stay quiet and move around the edges of the crowds, trying not to be isolated but also trying not to get noticed. It feels okay when we have a task to do, because everyone has something to talk about and we don't have to chat to each other about our interests or what we did at the weekend. Everyone else seems to be able to do this but I get lost and feel like they're talking a different language that

I don't understand or know how to join in with.

It's lunchtime that's the worst, our group is last into the lunch hall and it's loud and chaotic and everyone is already sat with someone they know. The hall is lively with chatter, and I don't want to be involved in any of it and so I escape to the toilet for as long as I possibly can. It's only when I re-emerge that I spot Maisie sat on a table looking unable to connect with anyone else, I quickly reach for some lunch and hurry to take the place next to her.

"Hi." I wave awkwardly on approach.

"Oh hi." She smiles, "How's it been so far?"

"Erm, yeah great." I lie and attempt to sit on the chair next to her.

"Oh, sorry I'm saving this for Grace." She glances at me apologetically and the girl next to me looks over her shoulder at me with a look of disgust then turns back to her friend and sniggers.

"I don't really have anywhere to sit." I mumble, pleadingly, tears beginning to spring in my ears.

"Look, there's a space over there, some of the girls on that table are really nice." She gestures to a table with one space left, full of girls who already seem to have formed a good bond. I rise from the table, giving Maisie a weak smile and wander over to the table.

"Can I sit here?" I say meekly, all of the girls stop their conversation and turn to look at me, from my white, tennis trainers to my peach top. They return to the chatter without so much as acknowledgement of my words, I don't know what to do so I stand there waiting and waiting, until a girl turns around and gives me the evil eyes and I know I'm not welcome at this table. Everyone seems to be staring now, staring at the girl who has no one to sit with and this is exactly what I feared, mum is never going to be allowed to send me anywhere like this ever again, I don't care if I've promised. Eventually, I find a free seat and attempt to eat my soggy tuna sandwich, trying not to cry as tears fill my eyes and all I really want is to be back at home with Basil, Scruffy and Anna.

*   *   *

Today is the day, it's my taster day at Southly and we've been told to take our swimming costumes to try out the pool. I'm so incredibly nervous but mum has taken me on a few drives to the school now so I know what it looks like and I feel like the map I drew of the school will help me not to get lost. I've been thinking about today a lot, and I've decided that I'm not going to let what happened at Westgate Girls to happen at Southly; today I'm going to be H. I will attend my new school as H, and everyone will love me and I'll be the most popular girl at school because I'll be cool and confident.

Mum delivers me at the door to the assembly hall, we're late as usual which is good because the activity has started and I don't have to worry about going up to people I don't know and involving myself in their conversation, because that is alien to me and I just can't do that without feeling silly. I'm put into group two, one of two groups, this taster day is smaller and I'm grateful of that. There are boys in my group, and I attach to them because I know that's easier than being with the girls. There's a brown, shaggy haired boy who reminds me of Alfie and a plump, ginger boy with freckles who seems funny, and I like being friends with funny people. Immogen is also in my group, who I know from tennis, we don't really speak to each other because I don't think she really gets me, and I don't get her but at least we have someone we know to lean on and pair up with.

The day is super fun and there are so many different activities and games to play, the best part is that it doesn't feel like we're being assessed and observed by teachers all the time, like at the other taster day. Swimming is our last task for the day, and I've been really looking forward to it all day so that I can show people how good I am and then maybe they'll want to be friends with me, I've brought my dolphin towel for good luck and everyone else seems to have more adult towels.

Mr Hill and Miss Wade assign us to our teams, I'm with the ginger boy, his friend who looks like Alfie and a tall, mousey-coloured hair, quiet girl called Amy, she's not good at swimming and it frustrates me that she's on my team. At the end of our swim, our teams have to compete in a rely, everyone else seems to want an explanation of this but I do not, and I get straight up on the diving board ready to take my turn first so I can get my team off to a good start.

"Hold on, young lady." Says Mr Hill, gesturing for me to get down, "I think we'll just start in the water today until we know everyone is okay with diving. So, boys, you start off first and then we'll go boy, girl, boy, girl. Okay first boy in the water, three, two, one." He blows the whistle and I wish he would just say 'go' do other people not feel how painful that sound is and how it echoes around the pool for ages afterwards? The ginger boy is in the water, and everyone is cheering him on, obviously he is well liked by everyone.

"Dinner, dinner, dinner." They all chant. That's it, I'm cool, I'm H, I'm going to join in with their chants and be one of them.

"Dinner, dinner!" I yell, cheering on my teammate, but everyone turns to look at me. Maybe I don't know him well enough to call him his nickname? Maybe I should call him Kyle like the teachers do? To be fair, it is a bit mean of me to call him a nickname that is clearly given to him because he eats a lot of dinner, when I hardly know him. I stop and let everyone else cheer him on.

It comes around to my turn, I make my way into the water and swim full pelt to make up some time that Dinner lost us (sorry Kyle lost us) in the previous lap. As I exit the water, I see everyone looking at me, confused maybe about how quick I was, there's a girl called Becky glaring at me from one side of the pool. Mr Hill said she is trying out for the Olympics in swimming and trains every morning before school, she doesn't look very approachable.

"Wow, you're fast." Says Ian, the Alfie lookalike.

"Thanks." I grin and turn to Kyle, "Well done, you swam well."

"Yeah, well done, Ginner." Ian says and slaps him on the back. So that was my mistake, his name is Ginner not Dinner, in relation to his ginger hair. Should I say something? Probably not, maybe they all thought I was saying Ginner, hopefully.

I don't come away from the taster day with friends for my first day, but I know that I could feel much more comfortable here making allies than I would anywhere else. I could fit in here, as long as I tried really hard to be H and not Harry.

22
'YOU GOT THIS!'

February 2022

It's a cold, Wednesday morning and I wake to the warmth of my sunlight alarm clock, which has adjusted my body clock through the winter months so that I don't wake in the dark, confused and half-asleep. The morning starts as it usually does, Meeno leaping across my head and licking my face, so happy that his human is alive after all that time of lying still. I allow him a quick cuddle before rolling out of bed and entering the bathroom, I must brush my teeth first so that I can wash the potential splats of mint off my hands before washing my face. It feels wrong if the order gets all mixed up and I have to start from the beginning. Meeno waits, sat by my feet as I ready myself, he knows that a walk is imminent and his little tail bats the tiled floor in quiet anticipation.

Next, I wet my hair and scrunch in some hair gel to set my curls, which I have now started to embrace since my autistic realisation. As a child I was always the curly haired one and everyone would tell me how beautiful my curls were, somewhere along the way I started to hate them because my hair wasn't straight like all the other girls. I literally neurotypicaled my hair! It has always irritated me when strands run across my face, and it never looked right being pushed back with a headband; now I segment three parts of my hair and clip them back from my face to keep stray hairs from falling onto my skin. It feels refreshing to find a haircut that makes me happy every morning.

My work wardrobe is limited, I've always favoured comfortable clothes that are loose on my legs and arms but would often put myself through discomfort just to be stylish. Now, I accept that flares will always be part of my wardrobe, no matter the trend and I will never wear t-shirts again that put pressure on the tops of my arms, I shudder slightly at the thought. It's taken me to know I'm autistic to understand that wearing clothes that were scratchy and tight caused my emotions to be all over the place. I wish I could wear the same outfit every single day to work but alas, I don't want to look like someone who never washes and doesn't care about their appearance. I'm starting to consider buying the same trousers in all colours of the spectrum so that I know I'll be comfortable, wearing the same thing but no one will ever know.

Every morning, Meeno is walked up the road by our house, in any weather so that he's worn out for being left on his own until his dog walker picks him up later in the morning. He's often sleepy and walks at a slow pace, needing reminders to hurry up so I'm not late for work. When we return home he's hyperaware that he will be left alone any minute and sticks to my side in the hope he can escape out the front door with me. Either that or he hides himself away under the kitchen table, trying to conceal himself enough that I forget to put him in his crate.

"Bye baby!" I blow him a kiss as I lock the front door

and peer at him through the living room window. "Love you."

At work, our office is usually full when I appear on a morning, never being one for good time-keeping skills and I breeze through the door with a big smile, no matter the events of the morning. Home is home and work is work, they have separate boundaries and so I don't usually bring the emotions of one into the other. People have often asked me how I can cope with so many safeguarding issues in my job and go home to sleep at night, I guess that's where being autistic is helpful. I can detach myself from the emotions of others and the events outside of my immediate environment because they're not in front of me; they're out of my timeline.

As a young girl, I didn't consider that other people's lives continued outside of mine, it wasn't that I thought their lives stopped as soon as I stepped out the scene, but more that I just never presumed there was anything outside of what I experienced. I only realised this wasn't the case when I had my had my first boyfriend, one day lying on his chest I felt his heart beat and realised that he was real somehow. The more he talked, the more I understood that he had his own thoughts and emotions that were separate to mine and he had experienced things before I came along. At home, I'd never asked my parents what they did at work all day or about their emotions and what they had done with their lives before I was born. Of course, I'd seen pictures of when they were younger and they'd mentioned things they had experienced in life previously, but I never really connected with that, it was distant somehow.

As I walk into the office, the mood lifts and everyone turns to welcome me into work. My team is incredible, they're all individually lovely people who I connect with and work with so well, together we have the same opinions on practice and the systems in place. I certainly wouldn't have managed so well in my current role without the support and appreciation of my colleagues that I can now call my friends. Throughout my days at work, I have learnt that I'm unable to write notes or reports when other people are talking, it's impossible for me to tune out of their conversations. There's absolutely no hope for me making phone calls when other people are around because the anxiety of them speaking and me not being able to follow the conversation, I'm having on the phone is too much.

Helen approaches me for a discussion about one of the children, whilst everyone else continues with their morning duties. During the conversation, I zone out and look around the room seeing everyone busying with their typing, completely able to switch off from the conversation I'm involved in. Jo rises from her chair and approaches Lizzie at the other end of my desk and begins to whisper about a report they are working on together. And just like that, I can't listen to Helen anymore, my brain is flitting from her words to Jo's and it's all a jumbled mess.

"Is it okay if we go in the other room?" I ask Helen, who willingly agrees, "Sorry, I just can't listen to someone if there's background noise that's all." We access the room next door and continue our discussion. In my previous work environments, I wouldn't have advocated for myself to meet my needs by moving out of the room, I would have just carried on, struggled with the conversation and never said what I wanted to say in response. Each day, I'm learning how to meet my needs in the workplace and shout a little louder about what I need. I don't see myself as being difficult quite as much now, I try to see it as that I am disabled, which means I am unable to process information fully if there's noise and that's okay and I should be given reasonable adjustments as a basic human right.

Becoming a self-advocate in such a short amount of

time makes me feel stronger than I ever have. I finally feel like I've found my voice and that I'm opening up so many doors for myself. I try every day to help other neurodivergent people to advocate for their needs and to communicate what they want because their voices are important and deserve to be heard. I wish this version of me could be transported back to my childhood years, where I never asked for help because I didn't want to seem needy or when I just couldn't use my voice. I wish the older version of me could sit with little me and teach her all about what she needs to ask for and to not take no for an answer from anyone.

I no longer feel like I have to hide my struggles away from the world. I'm proud to have the differences I have and I'm even prouder when I make people aware of them and ask for barriers to be removed. It's not easy making sure people treat you with equality, in a society where people tell you to stop being a drama queen or a princess just because you need more help. It's not easy when society doesn't see invisible disabilities and discards your problems because you don't 'look disabled enough'.

Despite the passion I have for changing everything to support neurodivergent people on a daily basis, work is draining and by the end of Wednesdays I am ready for a rest. Tomorrow is a working from home Thursday, something that has saved my brain a lot of fatigue. I was granted permission to work at home once a week as a reasonable adjustment and it's been very welcome. Working part-time is hard enough but in my workplace, it's loud and chaotic and there's always people in and out of the office, having conversations all day, there is no way that I can write reports or training or get my notes done. On Thursdays, Meeno curls up on his bed behind me for most of the day, occasionally moving to sit on my feet when entering a deep sleep, so that he knows when I get up and won't leave him alone. We both like working from home, there are no expectations, time constraints and noise; we spend the day in blissful silence.

July 2022

Today is the day of our National Conference at work and I'm bricking it, I have been as soon as a volunteered to do a talk on Neurodiversity: Autistic Trauma and Neurodiversity-Affirming Practice. When the email came around asking for volunteers to present on the topic of neurodiversity, I couldn't not put my name forward, I had so much I needed to say and for other people to hear. Initially, Helen volunteered to help me and apply her knowledge of trauma to the topic, but she's been unwell and unable to make it into work for the week, so with just two days to go I had to re-write the presentation.

Lizzie offered to drive me and Amanda to the meeting and for that I'm grateful, it means I have an extra hour and a half to recite my script to make sure it's delivered perfectly. We meet outside her house at 7:15, and as always, I turn up five minutes late, anxious and annoyed at myself for my tardiness, sliding into the backseat of her van. I'm thankful that I managed to secure the backseat so I'm able to focus on my presentation on the drive and keeping up conversation isn't my responsibility as much as the person sat next to the driver. As soon as I settle myself in, Lizzie asks how I'm doing and offers me some breakfast in the form of honeycomb and flying sauces, which I reject politely, the thought of eating is a little too much right now.

"If you need to switch off and get into your zone, you're more than welcome to." She offers, "Also, if you need us to shut up and play some music so you don't want to interact with us that's equally fine."

"Thanks, I appreciate that. I do have a lot of work still

to do on the presentation, so I think I'll just put my headphones in and do my practice, if that's okay?"

"Sure it is!" Amanda smiles at me from the front seat, "If you need any help, just let us know." It's incredible to experience a drive with people who don't mind me switching off in the backseat, when others have always made me feel rude for needing silence and the safety of my headphones. I smile to myself and pull out my presentation materials, beginning to mutter my script under my breath. I'm so used to scripting my interactions with other people that doing presentations in that format feels right. It brings me comfort to know exactly what I'm going to say and the words I'm going to use, that way I don't veer off topic or forget which words to use and in what order. Through blogging and writing stories throughout my life, I've found that my written words are often more powerful than what I say and using that strength in my presentations is helpful.

An hour later I emerge from my zone, taking my Air Pods out of my ears and packing my things back into my bag, feeling more calm and confident. I begin to focus my attention to the conversation in the front seat, which is a sensitive topic being discussed between Lizzie and Amanda, for which I immediately feel like I'm intruding. I want them to know that I'm out of my presentation practice space and very present in their conversation but it doesn't feel right to interrupt and so I sit in the backseat waiting for the right time to ask a pointless question so I can integrate myself back into the interaction. Finally, the moment comes.

"How are we getting on?" I ask, making reference to the journey time and just like that I'm welcomed back into the conversation. We arrive at the venue twenty-minutes later and my anxiety spikes as I spot colleagues arriving in droves through the front entrance. In this moment, I'm so thankful for travelling with people I know because arriving at a place I've never been and entering a room of people I barely know is one of the most terrifying moments there is. The worry of choosing where to sit and waiting to recognise people is enough to raise my heart rate and make my stomach do flips.

As we enter the room for the conference my heart nearly stops, it's huge. There are about fifteen tables crammed into the space, the lights are bright and there's a sea of faces I've never seen before. It hits me like a truck just how many people are going to be in the room, watching my presentation, all their eyes on me and I suddenly feel like I can't breathe, the air has been knocked out of me. Amanda and Lizzie glance towards me, measuring my face for signs of distress and anxiety, I must look wide-eyed and pale because Lizzie offers me encouragement as we sit down.

"It'll be fine, just try and pick something out on our table that you can focus on. You'll smash it." It takes me four trips to the toilet to settle, feeling nauseous and unable to determine whether I need the toilet or if it's just nerves, which reminds me of the same predicament I had during my high school exams. I return to the table following my fourth toilet trip to a note on my place setting from Lizzie, *You got this!* and I stow it away for my memory box, touched by the gesture, unable to articulate how much that means to me.

After an hour of introductions, it's my turn to present to the group, I'm first up and for that I'm thankful, I'm happy to get it out of the way. Slowly, I gather my presentation notes and make my way up to the front of the room, the back of the room feels miles away and everyone's eyes are on me, all of which I avoid as I arrange my PowerPoint on the big screen, which reads: Neurodiversity – through the eyes of semi-speaking neurodivergence.

"Hello everyone!" I announce to the room, hoping the people at the back can clearly hear me. "Today I'm going to be presenting about autistic trauma and how we become neurodiversity-affirming professionals. Just before I start, I wanted to note that I can become mute when overwhelmed and I'm really hoping that doesn't happen this morning, but if it does, please bear with me." I explain the impact of late diagnosis, what autistic trauma looks like and the medical model versus the social model that our healthcare professions use. During the presentation I discuss sensory processing trauma as part of being an undiagnosed autistic.

"I have a very clear memory of being a baby, which I know is hard to believe, and my family members are holding me down to put cream on my nappy rash, I know a lot of information! I remember the feelings as I speak about this, as if it were happening right now. Because of having tactile sensitivity, it was incredibly distressing for someone to rub my body with horrible smelling and feeling creams that I could not escape from or verbalise why I was having such an intense reaction. For years after that experience, I would feel anxious every time I entered my bathroom because the tub of Sudacrem they used was placed on top of the cabinet and I wouldn't be able to take my eyes of it the whole time I was in there." As I retell the story, I see the faces of people in the audience, visibly shaken by what I explain, some look emotional and I know I've hit the mark of what needed to be said to explain the sensory experience and pain.

The presentation is over in thirty-minutes, and I turn to the organiser to ask if we have time for any questions, which she states we have five minutes for.

"Okay, we have time for a few questions, but just to let you know I can struggle to process questions in the moment so I may need you to email some of them for me to answer fully." I smile, happy that I have self-advocated without feeling ashamed or apologising. Before each question, the audience members congratulate me on a fantastic presentation that's given them lots to think about.

I'm asked about the difference between independence and autonomy, my thoughts on certain therapeutic resources and future directions of the work we can do on neurodiversity. One person asks about the diagnostic process and whether the current assessment tools are effective.

"I think every autistic person's assessment is very different, which I've found from talking to and listening to the neurodivergent community. Personally, I completed an interview-style assessment, which was both with me and my parents and I gave the clinician that much information that I didn't need further assessment. I think I gave them a ten-page document of information on why I was autistic, so really at that point they really should have known." The audience laughs and I relax explaining the different assessment routes and what others' experiences have been. I feel confident, knowing I've answered the question appropriately and they heard what they needed to.

Questions are ended and the audience erupts into applause, I feel my cheeks burn, praise is hard to take. For the next twenty-minutes, person after person approaches me to congratulate me and thank me for my insight and bravery of opening up about my own experience and start to share their professional experiences, as well as their questions around their family members 'potential neurodivergence'. I feel on top of the world, knowing that my words have started a change, just what I dreamt of from the experience.

At the end of the day and after much questioning, acknowledgment of the emails I will be receiving from people wanting to know more and thanks from people, I slide into the back of Lizzie's van, exhausted. A headache plays at the depths of my head and I nervously eat my snacks, which I hadn't been able to until we left the venue. Immediately, Lizzie recognises my distance and turns to face me as she starts the car.

"I can't imagine how much that whole experience has been for you, it's been a lot to process and all the social aspects, questions and attention. Please feel comfortable being silent and just listening to us or put your headphones in if you need to. Please don't feel you have to speak, save your energy." I'm not sure what to say in response, this is the first time someone has recognised my need for distance and to disconnect from speech without me having to say a word. For the first time, someone else has recognised exactly what an experience has been like from my perspective and offered me the support and accommodations I need, without me having to advocate or hint. I honestly feel like I've never been more understood as I sink back into the chair, relaxed, free of the constraints of speech and listen into the conversation between my colleagues, laughing as they joke around.

*   *   *

Arriving home from the long day of exhausting masking, I reach for my phone and type out a text to Lizzie:

Can't actually express how much it meant for you to offer me space to just shut off and be mute in the car on the way home. It may seem like a little thing but please know that it means a lot and it's not something I've experienced before from people!

She responds almost immediately:

Perhaps other people haven't been as lucky as I have in getting given a presentation on what their friend has experienced and how things have made you feel.

You can be such an insightful, supportive, happy, fun energy to be around that it's easy to want to keep you talking as you bring so much to a conversation but after discussions we've had lately I know that would be me being selfish... that as someone who cares about you I knew I needed to give you that space. I also feel comfortable in your presence to share a prolonged silence so if you ever want to do something without words/eyes contact etc that's cool. Plenty of stuff like dog walks, crafts, food, cinema and such that doesn't need words.

It's in that moment, receiving that text that I feel more connected to the younger version of myself than I ever have. Everything she said about me was who I was when I was little Harry, so full of energy, so much to give and so much playful comedy but constantly told I was 'too much'. I suppressed so much of that part of myself, but by starting to unmask in my working environment, people have been able to see those aspects of me that no one has seen for a really long time. But this time, no one has told me to dim myself down and become more like everyone else, I've been told to be just as I am and not to change and that feels so far removed from everything I experienced as a little girl. I shed a tear, thinking of the little girl who hated who she was, constantly embarrassed by how she acted and tried to change herself to fit a mould that didn't exist but stifled her creativity and natural charisma.

Sitting here in my living room, Meeno curled up on me knee, I wish I could transport myself back in time and whisper in the ear of the girl who put her daddy's wellies on up to her knees to make everyone laugh and tell her to never change. I want to tell her that people will love you one day for your differences, and you'll bring something new to the world that's special in all the best ways. I wish she knew her quirkiness was the best part of her, her ability to deviate from the norm wasn't a weakness, it was a strength. She knew her own mind better as a five-year-old than she ever could at twenty-five, she was bold and brave and kind-spirited, with all the willpower to overthrow all the negativity, had she been allowed to flourish in her individuality. I realise that I can't wait to get back to the core of my identity, because those are the very best parts of who I am.

23
MY ALEX & BASIL

2005

Alex is explaining atoms to me, they sound intriguing but then everything does when it comes out of my brothers' mouth. I hang on every word as he tells me that the coffee table is made out of lots of atoms, and they all vibrate against each other. I don't know what this means but he's enjoying telling me so much and it's time with my brother so he could literally be telling me anything and I would listen.

Alex is eight years older than me, meaning that he's nineteen and he's just started studying physics at university. Alex hardly ever comes to visit now, and I really miss him, when he tries to leave I tug on his jumper, attempting to pull him back into position where he should be, at our house every weekend.

Alex is my half-brother; we have the same dad, both with dad's darker hair colour, messy eyebrows, thin lips and a smatter of freckles across our faces. Neither of us are particularly tall for our ages and all three of us have the same quirky sense of humour. Although Alex makes dad laugh more and I don't like this, I want to be the funny one everyone laughs at. I would do anything to hear the two of them laugh; it's my very favourite sound.

Alex used to stay in the front bedroom of the house but now he sleeps next door to me because it has a double bed instead of a bunk bed. Mum and dad said that I must sleep in my own room when he comes to stay but this is rubbish because I want to be next to Alex at all times whilst he's here. He has a girlfriend at home called Rhian, who I really like and sometimes they come to babysit for me but since she's been in the picture, Alex has visited us less and less. Now he's at university he goes home to see his mum and girlfriend most weekends, so I don't get to see him much and that makes me cry when I'm on my own in my room. I don't really know much about Alex' life, I've never been to Alex's house, never met his friends and don't really know his mum. That feels really strange when he knows everything about me and has met all of my friends. I can't really imagine what he does when he's not here, but he always talks to dad about people I don't know and don't really care about, they seem to have a secret code and I want in.

Last week, we went to visit Alex's new student house on the way back from my tennis competition in Hull. His house was very small and his room even smaller, in the bedroom he hid an airsoft gun and I begged for a go with it, dad placed a helmet on my head and the massive gun in my arms, they both laughed at the ridiculousness of my size compared with the huge gun and helmet. I wanted to stay in that room for hours and explore my brother's new life, with all his posters and worksheets scattered all around. I was taken in by his stories of his housemates – Downstairs and Upstairs Dan and Richard, all the funny things they have done in the early hours of the morning and an incident with a frying pan that I didn't get but dad seemed to find hilarious. I've never been where Alex has lived before and I wanted so badly to learn more about this part of his life and who he is when he is not with me. It never really occurred to me that Alex existed outside of our weekends together and that he had other people in his life that are important to him that I don't know. I start to feel like maybe the more important people he has in his life, the less he will think about and love me. It's bizarre to me that I have no knowledge of his life outside of me, and I wonder whether I've ever asked him about himself.

I never ask anyone about themselves outside of what I see and know, I don't know what dad does when he's at work or what mum does all day whilst I'm at school. I don't know about their lives before me, unless they tell me things. I don't know much about anyone other than who they are to me. It made me sad, standing in my brother's new bedroom, that really, I know nothing about him.

* * *

Today, we are taking a family photo to send to Grandma Australia because I write to her on my birthday and at Christmas and they always send her some photos with my letters. I'm wearing my purple jumper with love hearts on, some jeans and mum has braided my hair with my favourite purple hair-bobbles. The jumper is scratchy, so I nibble a carrot to make myself feel better, which includes eating around the core and leaving the best bit until last. Alex laughs at me and points out the orange stain around my mouth. Mum isn't pleased since we are taking photos.

She picks up the camera and organises me, dad and Alex on the floor, Alex and dad resting on their arms, sat upright and I weasel myself in between them, underneath their arms, my favourite place to be. I love rough and tumble with dad and Alex, they don't hold back like a lot of the boys at school do and fight with me as they would anyone else, I like to be treated like one of the team. I pull Alex's ear and he starts to chuck me over his shoulders, spinning me around and swinging me about trying to shake me off his, now red, ear. I'm giggling loudly, enjoying the moment of closeness with my big brother and loving the attention, the spinning and the climbing.

Suddenly, Alex loses attention of our game, his phone vibrating in his pocket, puts me down and answers the call, taking himself off into a different room. I follow his steps to the closed door, listening to his conversation, he's laughing and talking in hushed tones to someone, probably Rhian. As he starts to walk towards the door, I overhear him telling Rhian he loves her and then they're arguing about who loves each other more.

I feel a prick of jealousy; my brother doesn't tell me he loves me. In fact, none of our family really talks about loving each other, we very rarely hug or share our feelings. Maybe that's something I want? Maybe it's not, I'm not sure. All I know is that I want to be my brother's favourite person and not Rhian, because he is and always will be my favourite person. Just this week, at school they asked me to describe my two favourite things and I picked Basil and my brother, I described his dark hair and what we do together, but I didn't write anything about *him*. I only wrote what I knew of him; I know that he likes Coca-Cola because that's what he always drinks when I see him. I know he likes video games because that's what we play together. But I don't even know what his favourite colour is or what his friends are like. Maybe Rhian knows all those things about him and that's why he loves her the most.

Alex is not just 'Alex', he's *my* Alex. Whenever I talk about him, I call him my Alex and people find that weird but it's not. When I'm talking about mum and dad, I say my mum and dad because then they don't get confused with their mum and dad, it's the same for Alex. He's the best Alex there is and he's my Alex and I don't want anyone else to confuse him with their rubbish Alex. My Alex taught me how to ride a bike, play video games and shoot a water pistol, Alex has been my first friend and understands me just as I am. Alex is patient when I distract him from his games or when I ruin his Lego buildings. Alex teaches me about things he's learnt in school and asks me about what I'm learning about in school. Alex phones me while he's not at our house just to check I'm washing behind my ears and to ask how my day is. My Alex is the very best Alex and no one else has a brother quite so good.

Someone who is almost as good at understanding me as my Alex is Basil, my collie-cross dog. He's a medium-sized dog, with a shiny black coat, brown sock marks around his feet and two brown eyebrow marks above his brown eyes. Basil comes with me everywhere and he is my favourite thing about being home. He welcomes me through the front door with open arms every day and I'm so jealous that mum gets to spend all day with him when she works from home and I'm at school. Mostly, I love the time spent with Basil in the outdoors, exploring new parts of the fields and making up stories whilst in the places they are set in, including forests and greenery. The best thing about Basil is that he doesn't need me to talk, he doesn't expect me to share, and he does as he is told. I want to take him everywhere with me because then I always have something to start a conversation and can use him as an excuse to escape a social occasion too.

We searched for a dog for a couple of months before finding Basil, the dogs didn't match our busy lives and my parents having a young child, but we really wanted to rescue. At the NSPCA shelter nearby, we were introduced to a collie that had just had a litter of puppies, with only one remaining at the shelter. Mum and dad were convinced that they wanted an older dog so that they didn't have to do too much training, especially with me taking up most of their attention, but they agreed to take a look. The dog trainer brought through a sleepy, black puppy in the crook of his arm and told me to sit cross-legged on the floor, placing the sleepy puppy in the nest of my legs. Immediately, his eyes blinked open, and his tiny mouth gave a cute little yawn, he looked nowhere else but my eyes and I was in love instantaneously.

Stretching his little limbs underneath my hands, he climbed my chest and licked me, cuddling into me with some much love and excitement. He was the one, I knew it and mum and dad did too, I turned around to see them signing a form to take him home. The next few weeks he was constantly manhandled and wasn't left to himself for more than a minute, he was the friend I'd never had because there was nothing silly I could say and do that would make him love me any less. A special interest in dogs was born and he was all I could think and talk about.

Mum and dad had always been convinced that I would request a cat rather than a dog. I had always been obsessed with cats, pretending often that I was a cat. Many of my days had been spent with me crawling around the floor, meowing and drinking water from bowls on the floor. I loved every moment of being a cat and as soon as I returned home from school, cat mode would be activated and there would be no conversation, just one 'meow' for "yes" and two 'meows' for "no", it was a great communication system that made me happy. Happy until mum told me I was getting too old to be cat all day and I needed to grow up. Instead, I would wear my cat mask around the house and out of the house whenever it was allowed, if I couldn't move and talk like a cat then at least I could hide behind the mask of one. I loved the mask, it hid my expressions, my voice and my eyes, no one wants to talk to a girl in a cat mask!

24
A COCKERPOO & AN IMPORTANT CALL

January 2022

I've felt like I've been waiting for this moment for so long and its finally here. In five minutes, I get to call my brother and tell him about my diagnosis. Alex is probably the person I've been most looking forward to telling because he was the person who always understood me and accepted me for being one hundred percent myself. He was the first person I texted after I received the news and I suddenly feel very emotional at the thought, blinking back the tears that have appeared in my eyes.

Alex's job means that he's away often and so it's been nearly a week since my diagnosis and I've not been able to speak to him until today. I don't tell him why I'm calling, instead I've told him it would be great to speak to him and when he didn't respond to my message I added 'P.S. it's important'. I start to wonder if he thinks I'm pregnant or getting married as the call waits to connect.

"Hey sis!" He answers the Facetime call merrily. He's sat in a rented room due to being away for work and I begin to question him about all of the items in his environment. We talk about his work trip and how he's feeling about being away from home and finally I can't hold it off any longer.

"So, I have news." I announce with a big smile, "No I'm not pregnant or getting married. I've been diagnosed as autistic five days ago."

"Oh!" He says causally, as if this is not a surprise, I briefly wonder whether dad has let it slip to him. Slowly he beings to smile, "well that makes a lot of sense. How do you feel about it?"

" I'm doing great actually, it feels a massive relief to finally understand myself and all of the things in my life that never made sense. Especially all the sensory stuff, like that I can't deal with messy hands and noises and people touching me. It's a lot to process and a lot to get used to though, I think it's going to take a while to get my head around."

"Well, it doesn't change who you are at all. You don't need to change, just be yourself because you've always been ace. I'm proud of you, sis."

"I know, I'm feeling really positive about it, I feel like I can be more myself now and I've already signed myself up to a talk for a charity about it all. I feel like I'm ready to use my voice for the positive and make more people aware of what autism looks like in girls and women." I say as Alex smiles.

"You'll be great at that."

"I was just so excited to tell you because I always felt like you were the only one that got me and let me be myself around you. You were always so patient and even when I was annoying or overbearing you were just so calm and lovely with me. You've been the best big brother and I really appreciate it." Alex looks away briefly, I can tell what I've said has made him feel a bit emotional.

"I wouldn't say I was that patient." He laughs, "But I'm just sorry that we didn't get to spend more time together growing up, I'm sorry for that."

"Alex, there's eight years between us, you had university and a girlfriend and so much other stuff going on, it was always going to be like that. Having different parents meant we didn't get to spend a lot of time together." I reassure him but really, I wish we had had more time together and I still wish for that now, with him being so far away and me being absolutely incapable of keeping in touch with people or visiting.

"With that in mind, do you think dad's autistic too?" He smiles and I laugh, and we discuss dad's many habits and the unusual things he does and ways that make us both love him so much. Our phone call draws to an end, with Alex going to call my niece before her bed and me making tea, we usually end our calls with a quick 'bye' but today feels emotional and like we've reconnected on a level that we haven't for a while.

"Bye bro, love you." I say nervously, this is not something we ever really tell each other; I guess it's not a Richardson thing.

"Love you too, sis. Take care of yourself, bye." My eyes fill with happy tears as the phone call ends and I sit for a few minutes recollecting the call and the kind words he said. Our relationship is always banterous and playful, with some spikes of sibling rivalry, it's very rare that it's emotional and we speak about feelings, it's not in either of our comfort zones, just like our dad. I wish I was able to tell my brother just how much he means to me and how much I've always looked up to him and wanted to be just like him all of my life, how much I miss him when we don't see each other for months on end and how much I've always missed him when he didn't visit on a weekend.

Last summer, he visited mum and dad's house with his wife, Kathryn and little daughter, Fliss. Alex and I spent hours in the kitchen, enjoying our time together just the two of us making samosas and a curry, dad chipped in occasionally and we told him to butt out in unison. Alex on task has always been my favourite Alex, in the kitchen he shows so much passion and attention to detail, he's so animated and in his element and we communicate on a different level at these times. Working together in the kitchen you can tell we're siblings, we know how to communicate to each other without words and in ways that outsiders wouldn't understand, we laugh at private jokes and share stories. That day, Kathryn had told mum how much Alex thinks of me and that she loves our relationship and the care we have for each other. I never really realised that my love for Alex was reciprocated on the same level, until he started calling Fliss 'Harry'.

"I keep calling her Harry all the time," he says smiling at me and putting his arm around my shoulders, "you're both two little things that I love and have to protect." The comparison he made was one of my favourite things I've ever heard in my life, and it filled my heart with so much joy. That night, we played an old game he had introduced us to into the early hours of the morning, drinking wine and making each other laugh until our stomachs hurt. It was one of the simplest but most special days I've had.

As I pack away my laptop, I Facetimed Alex on, Meeno stirs next to me, signifying it's walk time and I pick him up for a cuddle, his little curly legs going floppy as he completely places his trust in me not to drop him. I smile into his fur and a little tear escapes my eye once again as I think of all the fond memories I have of my Alex. Meeno joined our little family in September; he's just over eight months old and has the most perfect demeanor. I quickly decided that Meeno would be an Emotional Support Animal for me and potentially a Therapy Dog for others. He's friendly, calm but also wild at times and gives so much love to his humans, including constant cuddles and closeness.

Jack initially was very resistant to the idea of bringing a dog into the fold because he didn't want the responsibility and I must admit Meeno is a big responsibility, however he quickly came around once I'd promised to not rely on him for co-pawrenting. Secretly, I knew that Jack would come around to being as much a pawrent as I would be because of his love for dogs. The day after Jack had agreed to have a puppy, I booked in to go and see a new litter of tiny Cockapoo puppies and begrudgingly, he'd joined me for an hour journey to Manhill.

"Okay, Harry but we're just going to look at them, we're not bringing one back with us today." He sighed.

"If we love one of the puppies we will be bringing it home Jack, what's the wait going to do?"

"Get our house sorted and the things we need for a puppy and really think it through before getting one?" He suggested but it was wasted on me, once I have an idea in my mind there's no changing my plan and he's always been aware of that.

When we arrived at the house, we were immediately greeted by the smell of puppies, poop and wee; it was magical. All eleven puppies were in a pen in the living room, and all bounced around on top of each other in a desperate attempt to get to the new people entering the house, their possible new pawrents. I didn't know where to start, they were all so beautiful and giddy and furry and I wanted to take them all home. Before coming to see the puppies, I had my eye on two of the apricot pups, one being a little bigger than the other but I'd convinced myself that I needed to meet them and cuddle them all first before diving straight into taking home the cutest of the litter.

Jack settled down beside me on the floor and encouraged me to take one puppy at a time out of their cage whilst he had watched them all to see if there were some better behaved amongst the bunch. I was not looking at their behaviour, I was enthralled by their tiny, fragile bodies, wide eyes, happy tails and soft fur. Stroking soft things has always been something that's regulated me. My dad and I would often walk around shops in search of the 'Ultimate Softness' whilst mum trawled aisle after aisle dragging us along.

"That one there looks really calm." Jack had said, pointing to a docile little apricot puppy, one of the ones I had been intent on taking home. He wasn't too shy that his siblings were treading on him but not making too much fuss that he couldn't control his little body, like some of the others. I plucked him out of the mass of struggling pups, scratch marks had marred my hands at this point. His body completely relaxed as I held him and his little eyes met mine with absolute adoration, immediately I had known this was the one, just like I had known with Basil. I smiled at Jack, which let him know that this was the puppy we would be taking home, to which he had smiled back in agreement. After holding the little pup himself, Jack whispered to me.

"If you're going to get one, this is the one to get. He's lovely and calm." He smiled, as he looked down at the ball of fluff in his lap, as he had scrambled towards me, eager to get to his new mum already. The car ride home had an aura of excitement, Meeno on Jack's lap, whom he had stoked repeatedly, in between minutely checking for wee. We called both our parents on the way home to tell them the news and to ask my parents for their dog crate and puppy supplies. That first night was one of the best of my life, I knew I'd made the right choice bringing a puppy home because finally, my house had felt like a home for the very first time and I had felt like a little family unit overnight.

Meeno has continued to be the best additional to our little family, he goes everywhere I go, to tennis, on holiday, to restaurants and he's always so well behaved. Of course, there have been times where it's been exhausting training a puppy and the many sleepless nights but I've found a best friend who loves me silently and without judgment. He knows when I need cuddles and comfort, as well as when I need silence, he recognises my mood and adapts to it, placing his paws on my chest and making me smile each and every morning. He gives me zero space but for that I am glad, I always wanted to have someone alongside me but not on top of me or talking to me or constantly needing me.

I feel like I needed Meeno to understand how to be a better parent, as silly as that might sound. Being autistic, I've always struggled with regulating my emotions, resolving conflicts and being aware of my tone and actions, Meeno teaches me what is a kind and calm parent, he's great practice. No matter what, he will be always just like a little child to me.

25
GARETH GATES & BACON CROISSANTS

2002

We're going on holiday to France with Linda and her parents and Lee and Jonny and their parents, we're all going skiing, and I've never done it before but Linda and I are so excited and have been for weeks. We're both a little annoyed that the boys are there but we'll stick together. Linda and her parents are meeting us in France because her dad is a pilot and gets extra special flights, me and my parents are flying with Lee, Jonny and their parents Ang and Mr Alan. I like to annoy Mr Alan and me and Linda stamp on his toes whenever we see him. Mum and dad once asked me if they ever died who would I want to go and live with and I said Ang and Alan because they're both really funny and nice to me. They told me that of course I would probably have to live with grandma and grandpa but asked me if I would like to be with Aunty June and cousin Izzy and that was a firm *no* because I have to put my mask on whenever we see dad's side of the family. I don't really know why they asked me that question anyway, parents don't die until you get older and become an adult with your own family, so that was just a pointless conversation.

We wait in the airport waiting room, lounging around until our flight is called. I absolutely hate this bit of the holiday, it's the worst having to wait with no idea of how long I will be waiting for. I regularly ask dad for updates of when we will be getting on the plane, and he gives me the same exasperated look each time.

"I don't know Harry, I know as much as you do right now and as soon as I know I will tell you, so you don't need to keep asking." He says in an even voice, trying to stay calm and not let me know he's annoyed, I already know so I don't understand why he's pretending. I don't understand why everyone else isn't bothered about when we are getting on our flight, they just sit around happily chatting and snacking. I can't snack because what if I open my packet of sweets and they call our flight and then I have to rush to put my things away and then I'll get stressy feelings and it will ruin the holiday. I keep my belongings firmly in my bag to avoid this. It's okay if I know how long I will be waiting for because then I can estimate how long until I need to pack my things up and I won't be caught off guard by moving to a new location with different people and communication requirements, like handing over my passport and saying "hello" to strangers. Time is very important to me and no one else seems to care right now and even that is giving me stressy feelings because I don't know what to do whilst I wait.

Finally, after what feels like forever an announcement is made and dad tells me to hurry along because that's our flight. I can't listen to announcements in shops and airports and things like that, well I can hear it I guess, but I can't really take in the words they say because all the other noise makes it hard for the words to stick and they say it all in a very confusing way. I don't like getting onto a plane because there's always lots of unknown people you have to smile at and say things to as you board and they all expect you to be friendly and happy because you're going on holiday. I'm not happy when I get on a plane because these people look at me and smile when I don't want them to, and everyone is squished together trying to squeeze into their seats and there's lots of eyes watching you when you're not the first one on the plane.

We arrive at our seats and there's a middle-aged man with glasses and a balding head in the middle of our seats. Why is he there? There is no way I'm sitting in that seat if I'm next to a man I don't know, and mum and dad aren't next to me. What if he starts to talk to me and the words won't come out? What if he smells funny or touches my arm when he puts his arm on the armrest? What if he eats mushrooms next to me? I start to panic and grab mum's arm, pulling her away from the scary man and our seats. Knowing what this is all about my mum tugs away from me and leans towards the man.

"Hello," mum smiles at him, "would you mind if I sit with my daughter?"

"Of course." He smiles back at her, "Would you like the window seat?" He directs his question at me, and I freeze, looking at mum for reassurance and a voice. My eyes say 'yes' and she interprets it well.

"Sorry, she's a little shy, but yes we'd love to have the window seat please." It all seems so easy for mum to have this interaction with this strange man, and I wish it were dad that we were sitting with. We squeeze past the old man on the way to our seats and his left hand brushes my back accidentally on the way past, I shudder and immediately feel angry, I hate light touches the most, they make me feel all wrong. I don't always like sitting next to mum because she holds my hand when the flight sets off and she's always so sweaty when it does. I don't really want to be touched when I'm on a plane, but it makes mum feel better, so I close my eyes whilst she holds my hand and pray for it to be a quick take off.

I might not love the experience of waiting and getting onto a plane but I certainly love being on a plane. I'm not really sure what it is about the plane that I enjoy, maybe it's that no one is asking me to do anything and everything is in one place where I need it, I can get snacks if I want and use the toilet when I want. I love sitting in my seat, with my headphones in, reading a book or colouring or looking out of the window, it's soothing. It's better when mum and dad sit together because mum talks to dad instead of me and I can just be left in my little bubble to do as I please.

Flights are never long enough for me, I'm sad when we have to pack our things up and get off. All the chaos that comes with getting off the plane triggers stressy feelings again and mum helps me by waiting until everyone else has got off before we disembark. Just watching people frantically grab their bags and push past each other and the looks of stress on their face makes me anxious, I can see people being touched by other people and their luggage hitting them uncomfortably as they wade through the isle, it makes me squirm. The worst thing is when you have a bag on your shoulder, and you have to walk down an aisle and the bag keeps getting caught and ricochets off the armrests and hits you in the legs. That makes me all kinds of stressy. I never like carrying around bags and I don't understand why mum always wants a handbag with her, it's unnecessary and the word handbag just makes me want to cry, it sounds all wrong in my mouth.

Mum sometimes asks me to carry her handbag and I wish she wouldn't because it always smells perfumey and has makeup and other things I don't like in it. She asks me to get things out of it sometimes and I don't like the feel of anything in there, the tissues, the makeup, the handcream, it's all yucky! I wish she'd ask me to take her 'bag' not 'handbag' and then maybe I would do as she said. Lots of times I pretend I haven't heard her and turn my back so she won't ask me again, this makes her cross.

I'm carrying my rucksack today and that feels okay because I can carry it on my back, and it doesn't get in the way so much. I think when I go to big school, I'll take a rucksack for my books because the little homework bag we have to carry into school is annoying, I can only carry it in my hand and it hits my legs as I walk so I get really upset. It's also got a Velcro seal, and everything gets stuck in the Velcro and makes me all stroppy, especially if it's my hair, that's painful. Mum usually carries my bag for me and that feels nice.

Driving up to the chalet is a dream, there's snow everywhere even covering the fur trees that line the icy road we drive up on the way to the entrance. The taxi man tells us something in French and all the adults look at each other in need of some translation. Ang is the first to speak, she's an airhostess so I'm sure she knows bits and bats of languages. As we all unload from the car, I feel the air on my lips first, it's biting and bitter and I can't wait to enter the warm chalet with its roaring fire and comforting snacks.

In preparation for the holiday, mum bought me some ski Salopettes, which are red and black, they're very warm but I can't move much in them and that makes me feel very cross. The gloves on my hands were a welcome addition to my wardrobe, it means that I don't have to lick my fingers because they aren't making contact with anything, plus I couldn't lick them even if I tried! The thing I love the most is my bobble hat, mum said it doesn't go with my outfit because it's purple but it's cool because it's got rabbits on it and 'Harry' written on the front, that way people know what to call me and I don't have to introduce myself. We all dash into the chalet out of the cold air, all of our ski trousers making a rustling noise as they rub together.

Immediately, there is a rush of warmth beyond the snow, covered door and it's just as I pictured it, a cosy haven away from all the ice and snow. The windows in the kitchen stand ten feet tall and the balcony above hosts a hoard of icicles, each one more beautiful than any I've seen back home. In the corner of the living room stands an enchanting wood fire, the flames lashing at the glass frame that contains them. I'm enthralled the whole place is magical.

Stewart, the chef shows the adults around the chalet, indicating where to store things and which keys to use for which doors. Mum and dad beckon me to follow and show me to the room I will share with Linda.

"Now, there's a spare bed in our room if you would prefer to sleep with us?" She asks, pointing towards the bed in Linda's room and the bed in their room.

"Can I sleep in here please mum?" I plead, knowing that I will only feel panicked if I have to sleep with Linda, I'm not really sure why since she's my friend. Mum smiles and nods, stroking my hair gently. Lee and Jonny have bunk beds just outside of mum and dad's room and I stop to wonder if they mind sharing with each other.

*   *   *

Stewart is cooking a meal for everyone upstairs and I worry about what the different smells are as they slip under the door to the bedroom. Sometimes, dad cooks certain things, and I really can't go in the room or near the room because it makes me feel sick, I'm pretty sure it's when he cooks butter but I can't be certain because I've never got far enough in the room to see what's in the pan. Everyone has unpacked and has gathered upstairs to chat and play games, I just want to play on my own for a little while and Linda isn't here yet because her flight was delayed. I'm going to be with Linda all week so it's best for me to spend a bit of time by myself to get used to my new room and what to expect.

Mum says we have two chefs: Stewart and Andy, Andy is also one of the ski instructors. We have four nannies who will look after us in the day, who are called Gareth, Rob, Lou and Sammy, this scares me the most because mum and dad will leave me alone with new people all day and I worry that they won't be able to understand what I need or what I'm trying to say when my words won't come. I often say what I think people want me to say too and end up with things or doing things that I really don't want to do because I don't know what to say to make it stop. It'll be okay when Linda is here though because she always helps me speak to other people and will eat the things I don't want and introduce us both to new people. I can hear footsteps plodding down the stairs as I finish writing in my diary, dad enters the room and I slam my diary shut.

"Dinner's ready!" He announces breezily and scoops me up into his arms, carrying me giggling up the stairs and into the kitchen.

"Will I like it dad?" I ask between giggles.

"Don't worry, he's made something special for you." All of my worries melt away, dad understands. Tomato pasta with heaps of cheese is set in front of me, whilst everyone else is served some mushroom yuck and although I can smell the nasty foods I don't mind, because my parents have made sure those mushrooms go nowhere near me, I'm safe.

*   *   *

I wake to the sound of commotion upstairs, mum and dad are both missing from their beds and the light outside is bright, the clock reads 10:03. I cover my face with the duvet, knowing that Linda and her family have arrived, and I need to get myself into a happy and chatty state. Talking is super difficult on a morning and I often have to point and shrug when people ask me questions, sometimes it feels like my brain has not quite woken up, but my body is too far ahead. Today we are 'hitting the slopes' I guess that means we are all going skiing because that's what we came here to do, I've never skied before and everyone else has so I need to learn quick to keep up, I hate being left behind.

Sometimes, I really panic when I am last back inside after break time at school or the last to fall asleep when I share a room at sleepovers, I don't like feeling on my own and late, it brings all sorts of unhappy feelings, and my body wants to flap around. I organise the order of the day in my mind, first I'm going to have to go upstairs, turn on my voice and smile, eat some breakfast without compliant, get changed into my super restrictive ski outfit, say goodbye to all the parents and meet the nannies, which is scary and then go to the slopes for the day, where I don't know what to expect. It's okay, Linda will be there, and she'll tell me what to do and where to go and speak to people when I can't, as long as I have Linda it will all be fine. Footsteps find the floorboards outside the door and the handle begins to turn, I pretend to be sleeping because everything's easier that way, I'm not ready for people to hug me or speak to me this early in the day. I hear mum's voice and small footsteps next to her.

"Oh, she's still sleeping," mum whispers quietly, "I'll wake her up and she'll be upstairs for breakfast shortly, Linda."

"Okay!" Linda responds excitedly and skips back up the stairs, the bedroom door closes and mum approaches, stroking the hair away from my face. I wake every morning with a smatter of thick curls across my face and the rest of it as a bird's nest of top of my head, it makes dad laugh most mornings.

"Time to get up sleepyhead," she smiles, meeting my tired eyes, "it's late and you need to grab some breakfast before we go skiing." She doesn't expect a response and her slippers slide across the floor on her way to the bathroom.

The kitchen is crowded as I enter, everyone is sat around the breakfast table chatting and finishing up their full English breakfasts. Linda immediately spots me entering the room and runs over to me, leaping on me in a big hug.

"Finally!" She gives me a huge grin, "I've been waiting for you to wake up for ages. Our nannies are coming soon and then we're all going skiing, I can't wait to show you how to ski, this is all going to be so fun. Here, there's loads of breakfast left, there's eggs and bacon and toast."

"Thanks!" I beam back, "I think I'll have a croissant though, I'm not so keen on a big breakfast." Dad slides out a seat next to him with a plate already prepped with croissants. As I seat myself, he slides the bacon towards me and shows me a new taste sensation he's found, a bacon croissant sandwich. Mr Alan looks on with disgust, seeming like he might be sick when we both have a bite of the strange mix. I laugh and rub my tummy in satisfaction, the way that adults do when they try to get you to try something new, just to emphasise the point that it tastes nice when it really does not.

"Right, everyone," Linda's dad, Graham bellows, "it's time we all go out onto the slopes, get wrapped up kids, it's going to be cold." Two new people enter the chalet, Gareth and Sammy, our nannies, who introduce themselves to everyone before giving instructions to the adults of how to contact them in an emergency and all the boring stuff. Linda approaches me, digging her elbow into my side and whispers.

"I like Gareth, he's just like Gareth Gates, should we call him that?" Her eyes shine with mischief, and I love it, I love being in on the joke and can't help but engage in whatever mischief Linda is cooking up. We rush to slip into our ski outfits and part ways with the adults, I glance back at mum and dad as we leave the chalet, it's hard being apart from them, but as long as I have Linda it will be ok.

At the ski slope, we all rush to climb onto the ski lift and Linda quizzes Gareth on his love life and whether he's a singer as we ascend the slopes, all of which he seems to find very amusing. I like Gareth, he has a very friendly face and gives us all his attention, always asking if we're okay or need help with anything, he makes me feel safe.

Our nannies drop us off at the kids' club, which is based on the beginner's slope, where Andy takes over and teaches us the basics of how to ski. I can't listen to any of his words and instructions, instead copying whatever the other children do, which seems to work, and Andy always seems pleased with what I'm doing. After our day on the slopes, we retire back to the chalet with Sammy and Gareth, where they present a carousel of different activities, Linda and I settle on the arts of crafts and the boys engage in a video game. We both create a diary, mine blue and Linda's orange, we stick in an 'all about me' page given by the nannies, something I always love filling out.

All about me!
Name: Harry Richardson
Age: 7 and a half
Favourite colour: red
Favourite animal: horse
Who am I here with: Linda and Lee
What I like doing best: playing

My answers look strange when I look at my finished sheet, mum likes red, my favourite is actually blue, but I haven't put that because that's the colour boys like and I'm trying to be friends with more girls now, so I must like girls' colours. My favourite animal is actually a dog but Grace and Maisie both like horses and Linda is getting a horse soon so it will all make things a bit easier for me to make and keep my friends if I say horses are my favourite. The last question was hard, I don't really know what I like to do best because people always tell me what I should like, I should like spending time with my friends and playing games with them and going on school trips and sleepovers. Mum and dad are always making me go to swimming competitions and new kids' clubs and inviting friends round to play but I don't really want to do any of those things, and I always say that but they seem to think they know what I will like and what's best for me. I never like doing them when I've tried them, not really, I just pretend to make everyone else happy. I ask Sammy what the question means about what I like doing best and she smiles warmly.

"What makes you happiest?" She tries to clarify but that only leaves me more confused. I don't really know, I know what makes everyone else happy, mum likes to eat chocolate and sunbathe and read a book. Dad likes to play video games and fix things around the house. Grandpa enjoys football, roast dinners and talking about his sporting victories. Linda likes riding horses and making new friends and playing with dolls. I don't really know what makes me happy, sometimes I get really excited about things but then I get migraines and I don't like that. I sometimes get a bit confused about what I like and think that my favourite things are being quiet, a brand-new exercise book at school and tearing leaves into small pieces, but those are strange things to like so that can't be correct. I like making other people happy the most, I guess, so I look at Linda's answer and write 'playing'.

26
AN AUTHOR & A BOOKWORM

April 2022

The scrapbook is opened at page one, the best page in a notebook, a fresh start, something new and exciting to write about. Although, this time I'm not writing a make-believe story, I'm writing about me and who I am. I need to know who I am, who I really am without the mask. I've never quite been sure of what I like, I've forced myself to like things that everyone else likes in an effort to fit in that I've totally lost sight of my genuine preferences.

Mum and dad have lent me some of my old schoolbooks and photos so that I can get a better understanding of myself and who I was as a child. In the pile, a blue book pokes its head out above the others, and I pull it out from underneath the weight of story book after story book, 'France 2002' it reads, a whole twenty years have passed since that skiing trip I recall so vividly. I flick the page and my eyes settle on a stuck in piece of paper:

All about me!
Name: Harry Richardson
Age: 7 and a half
Favourite colour: red
Favourite animal: horse
Who am I here with: Linda and Lee
What I like doing best: playing

It takes a few minutes to register what I've read, and I spend the next few minutes in silence, unable to form the words in my mind that I need to make sense of it all. I was just seven years old when I'd successfully accomplished masking, probably way before. My heart sinks as I read 'favourite animal: horse', I was always scared of horses and the only reason I had put that was because Maisie and Grace loved horses and I was sitting next to Linda who also loved horses. Linda always has been and continues to be the most self-assured person I know, she knows exactly who she is, want she wants and what her preferences are. Linda is the best self-advocate I know and there I was sat next to a little girl, younger than me, fully aware that she knew exactly what to put down on that paper with no doubt, only certainty, whilst I, a whole year older hovered over the page not knowing the simplest of things a little girl should know. And so, I did what I knew worked, I copied the confident little girl next to me, then I kept copying because I thought that someday maybe I'll understand myself the way Linda did.

I turn back to my scrapbook and write: 'Who Am I?' In bold sharpie pen, then flick to the next page and write: *my favourite things.*

Being happy and comfortable with Jack, Italian food, being happy, neat handwriting, trainers, love, laughter, the sound of the ocean, hats, making people laugh, active adventure, Meeno, the love Meeno gives me, raisins, walnut whips, Munchies, blue things, Spanish, long journeys, Gin, unusual trousers, music music music, cream eggs, writing, Shrek, Fridays, Edinburgh, Christmas in December, sitting in silence with another person comfortably, the first page of a new notebook.

My least favourite things
Creams, lipstick, mushrooms, Facetime, phone calls, dry things, not being able to read people, warm brain, instructions and directions, vegetarian meals, upsetting people I care about, vaccing, being forced to talk, fireworks, sitting still, not knowing who I am, when food recipes change and it tastes different, sharing my food, theatre, yolky eggs, soggy things.

I turn the page again and write: 'me' in the middle of the page, surrounding it with all of the things that make me, me.

Golfer, Speech and Language Therapist, semi-speaking, daughter, girlfriend, dog mum, writer, hiker, autism advocate, blogger, weight-lifter, author, aunty, sister, mental health advocate… autistic, ADHDer.

On the next page, I write what I often heard about myself but try to push down: *bad traits.*

Thick, childish, unlikeable, fussy, picky, challenging, naughty, annoying, moody, weird, unfriendly, flaky, emotional, uncaring, controlling, inauthentic.

There are so many more words that cover the page and I want to rip it out and start again. I don't want these words that I'm not comfortable on a page, in front of me, it's hard to see them all. Instead of ripping out the page, I take a pen and underline all of the words that have been said about me that were really a misunderstanding of my communication, they were said because I was neurodivergent and no one knew.

I quickly finish the activity and realise that every single word I wrote down was never true about me, it was all a result of being neurodivergent and misunderstood. I mourn those years I've lost worrying about other people's opinions of me, so much that I morphed into someone else, that I didn't even recognise myself. I became someone else just to make sure I made everyone else like me and I didn't even like myself anymore. I don't want to dwell in the negativity, so I turn the page and write about something that makes me happy.

I love, love, LOVE music.

Ed Sheeran, Taylor Swift, Little Mix, Arctic Monkeys, The 1975, The Killers, Stormzy.

Music helps me to process my emotions – I focus on the lyrics and not the sound. Some slow, sad music doesn't evoke feelings of sadness, it makes me feel warm emotions and helps me chill out – maybe it's a form of stimming for me. Life without music is no life at all, it is singularly the best and most important part of my life. My favourite song to listen to is 'Shiver' by Lucy Rose. It gives me such lovely feeling because it's so beautiful.

An author and a bookworm

If only I hadn't been dissuaded from creative writing in high school, I'm pretty sure this would also have been a stable and constant part of my identity. I wrote (or started to write and never finished) so many stories. I've always been obsessed with words.

Reading is also very important to me and has saved me in so many ways over the years. Sometimes I need to get lost in imagination and immerse myself in other people's thoughts and emotions. I think that reading really taught me how to understand people and helped me to develop the mask and different characters I've assumed over the years.

Right now, I'm reading lots of books on autism and enjoying learning lots about myself and how that relates to other people's experiences.

I stick in the book photos of my childhood that make me smile, me in a large deck chair with my head in a book, unaware of anything around me. Me in my dad's wellies up to my knees, giggling. In another I'm stood on rock in my tomboy clothes, raising my hands into the air with a wide grin. When I was really little, I was sure of who I was and I was comfortable within that, I was a much better version of myself. I love the little girl in all the photos who was an absolute character, always smiling and making others laugh with her mischief. Her smile was contagious, so much that I smile as I look at them.

It seems that throughout the years, my identity became what other people wanted me to be and the mask I used to help me to survive in each environment I was in. At school I had a well-behaved mask, a girl who was shy but always fit in with what other people needed from her. At tennis she was an ultra-competitive, over-achiever. At university she was a party animal, who always had energy and a joke up her sleeve. At work she was conscientious and hardworking but didn't venture out of the confines of her role. It was only at home, with my family that I ever took the mask off and became myself.

What I realise now is that when I was myself, I was my happiest, I was at my best. I wore those spotty, boy's shorts, baseball cap and sunglasses with pride. I ran and swam and threw balls without a care in the world. I was among my most favourite and safe people, my mum, dad and Alex and I was accepted as myself, at least for the most part. I believed in my dreams, and I lived in fantasy worlds most of the time, blissfully unaware of the troubles of everyday life. I worked hard to be an author, without fear of failing and I never ran out of creativity. I was at my very best.

As I close the book for the day, I reflect that I'm only just scratching the surface of who I am and what it means to be me. It feels like a big first step to understanding myself and loving who I am. I feel better than I have done in a really long time, I feel happy knowing that I'm on a journey to discovering who I used to be before the mask came along. Before all the masking started, I was a really cool kid, who knew what she wanted, I wish I could get back to that quirky character who did just as she wanted without a care in the world. I'm ready to start taking the mask off, love the person underneath and show the world how to be more accepting of the authentic me.

27
A LITTLE, ORANGE TILE

2007

I'm sat with mum and Anna in the kitchen, Anna's been over to play all day and we've just taken Basil for a long walk in the summer sun. It's just one week before we start at high school and on our walk we skirted around the perimeters of her new school, her pointing out all of the buildings and what's in them.

"I wish you were coming to my school!" She had said, but we both know that wouldn't be for me, the overwhelming crowds and all the people I don't know but Anna does. My new school has been on my mind for the last few weeks, and it's been hard to think of anything else, between shopping for new shoes, uniform and stationery. I enjoyed the stationery part but not a lot else, we visited the second-hand clothing shops because the school uniform is 'very bloody expensive' as mum put it. I let the tailors rag me about, pushing pins in and out of the material, slightly touching my skin, the whole thing made me want to scream but I pushed it back in because I'm trying to be a good girl.

Mum asked the tailor to try me with some bigger blazers because she wants to make it last a few years and the thought of wearing this blazer for years has tears rimming my eyes, it's heavy and claustrophobic and I can't wait to take it off as soon as she drops me at the bus stop on my first day. The worst bit of the uniform is the tie and shirt, I'm used to wearing both, but these shirts are really tight on my neck and make me feel like I'm going to choke, I swallow slowly as the material presses pressure on my windpipe, fighting back the urge to be sick. I want so badly to be a good girl and be normal and not hit the lady who keeps jabbing pins in me and touching my skin with her nasty, long nails but every time she comes near me, I flinch away. Mum notices and tells me to stand still, I keep the scream suppressed.

When we return to the house Anna chats away to mum about the new classes she's going to take, and which friends are going to be moving up to the high school with her. Mum has been feeding her questions about it for the past half hour because really, I'm not present. I hear the words as they pass my ears, but they don't stay, they ricochet off the invisible bubble that's shrouding me, I can hear parts of what she's saying but it's all so quiet and distant and some of the words don't stick.

My eyes are focused on a singular tile, one of the orange ones behind the kitchen hob, it's got a slight crack in the right-hand corner and the grout between the next tile doesn't quite overlap with the orange one. I've studied every single part of this boring, orange tile but my eyes won't move they're fixed in position without any intention to move. I tell them to move, will them to move but the more I fight the deeper they stare. I try to think about my body instead so that maybe I can distract myself from the tile, but I can't move it either. There's a gone-cold crumpet in front of me that I've been reaching for for a while now, but my hands won't quite get there, I try to wiggle my fingers and two of the ten respond slowly and barely.

I want so badly to join in the conversation, but words have deserted me and the room around me feels so far away, like if I reached out it would move further away and so I give up and allow the silence and stillness to take over. There are many times this has happened and I know now I just have to wait it out and slowly the movement in my fingers will move to my hands and slowly, slowly I'll start to move from my set position, my eyes will detach from their focal point and I'll be able to laugh at all of mum's silly jokes.

"Anna's going now." Mum declares and gives me a slight nudge, the nudge has no effect, and my eyes only move from the tile to the crumpet, I start to count its holes. "Are you going to say bye?"

"Bye." The word leaves a slight crack in my mouth, it's more of a whisper and I start to feel tears prick my eyes. All I want to do is hug my best friend goodbye and run up the garden with her, giggling in excitement that next time we see each other we'll have so much to tell one another about our new schools. I suddenly start to feel a hot feeling that rises up my body and it feels like anger. Why can't I just do these simple things? Why does Anna have to have such a rubbish best friend who can't even look at her as she leaves? What is so wrong with me? I just want to be like everyone else and people tell me I am like everyone else but I'm not, I'm not, I'm *not!*

I want to kick and scream and ask for help but nothing in my body or my mind responds to what I want right now. No one else seems to see what is happening under the surface of my body, not even the panic behind my eyes that is represented as a vacant stare. I feel so alone in this internal state of chaos, a duck springs to mind, Mrs Howell told us that birds appear calm on the surface but underneath their feet are frantically paddling to keep them afloat. I feel like a duck, especially with my webbed toes and ability to swim, but unlike the duck I don't feel like I'm afloat, I feel like I'm drowning, and no one is going to throw me some armbands, I'm going to be stranded in the middle of the ocean to drown and be eaten by sharks, my worst nightmare.

I start to hear the clock ticking in the background and focus on the noise, trying to count how many times it ticks so I know just how long this state of paralysis is going on for, *seventy-seven, seventy-eight, seventy-nine*. One hippopotamus, that's what people say between counts, I replace it with save me. *Eighty, save me, eighty-one, save me, eighty-two please save me.* I want to run away but I don't want to be on my own, I want to escape this room, but I don't know where is better. I want mum but I also want to push her away. I want to be out of my body because it feels all kinds of awful, but I don't know what that means.

Anna waves goodbye as mum opens the door for her and follows her into the garden to ensure she's home safe. I fear her return and the scolding that's likely to come with it, she'll only ask me why I'm such a bad friend and I'll feel so much worse. I worry about the hot feelings inside me and what it means for mum when she returns. Am I going to throw something or hit her or slam a door? I'm not sure and I really don't like it because I know I'm going to be out of control of my body as soon as my limbs start to work. Mum enters the house and closes the door just as the feeling returns to my hands.

"Harry, what's wrong? You've had a lovely day with Anna and then you've barely spoken for the past hour." She crouches down next to me, and I worry that if she says the wrong thing I might hurt her; I want her to move away I can't predict what I'll do next. I can't use words yet, so I shrug and turn my face the opposite way. It's so hard when this happens because all I want to do is crawl into mum's arms and allow her to hug me, but my body moves in different ways and I end up shutting everyone out. She gently places her hand over mine and the feeling returns to my body, the red-hot feelings subside and I stop worrying about what my hands might do. Instead, I start to weep red, hot tears that sting as they make tracks down my face.

"Oh Harry, tell me what the matter is please." Mum begs, her voice sounding shaky with her own tears.

"Mummy, I just can't do it. I couldn't talk and I couldn't eat and move and I'm a bad, bad friend." I try to explain but the words don't match the feeling, I let out a frustrated growl and burst into a new set of tears.

"Explain it to me, tell me what you were feeling."

"Well, it's like a glass wall is there, I can't hear things properly and everything feels very far away, and my body won't work or do what I tell it to do. All my feelings are on the other side of the glass, and I don't really know where I am." Even that doesn't do it justice, but mum must understand because she pulls me into a hug and strokes my hair.

"It's all going to be okay." She whispers, with her lips pressed against my curly hair. I want to believe her but I'm not sure what will make all this go away. Dad returns home to see our embrace and smiles, this must be one of the rare days dad gets home to me not screaming at mum. Mum tells me to go upstairs and play for a bit, while dad tells her about his boring day at work, I don't argue, dad's work does sound very boring.

Upstairs, I open a book and start to write down a new story when I hear the voices downstairs through the floor. As I often do, I press my ear to the carpeted floor and try to pick out words from their conversation, some I can grab like 'Harry' and 'quiet' but most of it is in hushed tones so it must be about me and what I'm doing wrong. I think about the orange tile again and wonder if I'm the only girl in the world who does strange things like this and if mum and dad wish they'd had a different child, an easier one. Whenever I ask them this, they get very upset and say not to be silly and they wouldn't change me for the world but I don't understand how that can be when I make mum so upset most days and I make everyone yell at me because I never do things right. Sometimes I even think the dog doesn't like me much because I yell at him a lot when he doesn't do what I ask him, and I want to cuddle him more than he actually wants to be cuddled. If I can't even make my dog friends with me then what chance do I have at high school?

I try so much to be liked by everyone and I only end up pushing people further away and making them angry. I just want mum and dad to be happy, sometimes when I go to grandma and grandpa's I look at pictures of mum when she was younger and realise how much happier she was before I was born. She looked so carefree and smiley and now she gets angry really quick and looks stressed all of the time and even though she says it's not my fault, it really feels like it is. I try so much just to be good when I get home from school but then straight away mum asks me to do something, and I just explode. I try to say sorry with written notes and gestures, but dad says it's really important that I actually say the word 'sorry' and teachers always say that if you say sorry and you do it again, it means that you aren't really sorry. I am really, really sorry whenever I make mum and dad cross and upset but then I do it all over again without learning because my body just does things without my mind's permission. Nasty words sneak out sometimes and I don't even think them before they come out, they surprise me as much as they surprise mum and dad and I want to take them back and apologise immediately but my body is so stiff, and I can't do anything but get more angry and try to escape.

The neighbours two doors down have started to call mum 'Mrs Shouty' because they hear her yelling at me all the time and mum got told that they feel sorry for me because it mustn't be nice to be shouted at constantly. I really want to go and tell the Mr and Mrs Albert that mum is a lovely lady, but her patience is tested every day by a devil child, that they don't see because they only see smiley, polite Harry. Beth next door once told me that she felt sorry for my 'poor mum' because I would 'be the death of her', which I didn't really understand because I would never kill my mum and that gave me all kinds of worry feelings. I guess she meant that I'm awful and the stress I bring is making mum poorly. I wish the other neighbors knew it was my fault and not mum's too. Mr Albert has a very bad cough and I think he'll die soon so maybe it doesn't matter so much what he thinks of my mum. Whenever they're out in their garden I make sure that they know I really like mum by giving her lots of hugs and telling her she's the best mum in the world.

A lot of people have lots to say about my parents' parenting styles, everyone else seems to have their own ideas of how best to 'handle' me and my 'challenging' behaviour. Grandma always says that mum should just leave me to be late for school when I don't get up in time and that mum is just doing everything for me when she should be teaching me to be more independent. If mum did do that, I don't think I'd ever eat or get anywhere on time or even go to school with the correct clothes on the right way. I don't know what I'd do without mum guiding me and showing me how to look after myself. Sometimes, dad has to pull me out of my bed on a morning by my legs because he's asked me five times to get up and each time I just fall back asleep because I'm always so tired. They need to make sure I've got my swimming kit and my homework and my bag and my breakfast and my shirt isn't inside out, or I haven't missed my socks. There are some days I've nearly gone to school without knickers, which would have been a very big surprise for the kids sat across from me on the playground.

No one really seems to understand what it's like for our

family because all their kids seem to be able to do these things for themselves, their parents don't have to speak for them when they lose their words or make sure they dry themselves properly after swimming. I think my parents are the best there are in the world because I am really difficult to have as a daughter.

28
SILENT STROLLS & DICKHEAD DETECTORS

March 2022

I stand in the bedroom with a towel in my hand, paused and unable to move not sure of what I was supposed to be doing with the towel and unsure how I got here and what I was doing before. I'm in the middle of my working week and my brain has been feeling warm all week, which usually signifies that I'm in sensory overload or burnout. I just want to cry, no one told me that adult life was going to be this hard, that day after day I would walk into a room and completely forget everything I needed to do. So often I find myself stuck in the middle of a task, not sure what I started and will swap to do something else, constantly flitting between the two. I used to aggravate my parents so much when I did this because I could never stay on task just to complete one thing they'd asked me to do. I always felt like such a disappointment and burden because I could never quite do such simple things that were expected of me.

Jack enters the room and without a word, takes the towel from my hand, places it in its intended place and envelopes me in a hug. His arms wrap around my body in a way that holds me upright and allows me to pour my weight onto him. I didn't realise how much tension I was holding as I allow all of my weight to transfer onto his shoulders and suddenly the towel doesn't matter, and the stressful day doesn't matter, all that matters is that I can share a space with Jack without any need to talk. The feeling in my body starts to return, slowly from my hands and chest all the way to my legs and feet, where before there was no feeling.

He pulls away from the hug and takes my hand, pulling me downstairs and into the kitchen, there he points at the fridge and shrugs, a gesture that I know means 'what's for tea?' I shrug in return, and he opens the fridge, first pointing to the chicken and sweet potatoes meaning 'mango curry?' and next to the turkey mince and bacon meaning 'dirty Cajun rice?' He knows that both of these meals are my comfort foods and will always make me feel that little bit better, we also almost always have the same foods for tea each week so its predictable and both of us have the same favourites we can have time and time again without getting bored. I point to the chicken and smile, he smiles back then points his finger to his chest, makes a love heart with his hands and then points to me. I realise that this is what it feels like to be understood and loved unconditionally by someone and it feels so incredible to finally be accepted for my mute and shutdown self.

In this moment, I wish that my parents had been able to do what Jack is so naturally able to do now we know I'm autistic. He respects that I can't talk some days and so we communicate with gesture and facial expressions, almost in our own little language. I wish that it would have been okay for me to come home in a state of silence and a need for solitude without any pressure to do things on time or communicate with everyone in my space. Back then, without a diagnosis no one understood why I wasn't able to answer questions about my school day and I would scream and shout because I was being asked to do the simplest of tasks. Tears stream down my eyes as Jack continues to hold me, I cry for that little kid who was so misunderstood and tried so hard to make everyone else happy. I never knew I needed a hug so much in my life, I never knew another person would be able to understand me so clearly by just looking at me.

Our embrace ends as Jack stretches out his arms and holds me at arm's length, I can feel him looking at me but to meet eyes would be too painful right now. Instead, I look at his chest, how his tie is lopsided underneath his shirt collar and feel myself smiling. I might need and depend on Jack at lot, but he also depends on me. Every morning, he slides a pre-tied tie over his head and tightens it, he never learnt how to do it himself and every once in a while, he needs me to do it for him. I then think of the weekend before where he had no idea where the iron was, that you put water in it and even how to move it over his clothes properly, suddenly a laugh bursts out of my mouth and he stands further away, studying me closely with his eyes, he's confused by my chuckling. He knows not to ask right now, instead laughing along with me. I feel better knowing that I'm not the only one in this relationship that needs the other person and that brings me some comfort. Jack smiles and takes my hand turning to pull me towards the front door.

"Let's go for a walk." He demands, knowing I always feel better for a bit of fresh air and for the first time in a few weeks I don't resist. I let him guide me out of the door, collect Meeno's things and decide the route we're going to take.

"Go on then, infodump" He smiles, and his tone suggests no pressure, so I shake my head. I'm not ready to talk just yet, but I appreciate the sentiment that he's offering me an open ear for telling him all about a special interest. I've never been on a silent walk, and it unsettles me, I start to wonder if I should just talk for a bit but before I can Jack interrupts my thoughts.

"Okay, shall I tell you about my day?" He squeezes my hand in his. I nod in response, and he starts to tell me every aspect of his day from the moment he woke up. I like the feeling of him infodumping his whole day, it brings me comfort that in the future I can do the same. I also really like to know what he's doing when I'm not around and what his thoughts and feelings are across the day, it's an insight I've never had about him because asking these things always seems the last thing on my mind.

I start to zone out of the conversation midway through and tap his shoulder, reversing my hands in a circular motion meaning 'go back'. He gets it and goes right back to the start of the day; I start to laugh.

We stay like that for the whole walk, him giving me information and me adding to it with a mix of sign and gesture, I make a mental note that I need to teach him the basics of sign so we can communicate like this more often. The thought makes me feel warm inside, this is what I always wanted, and it feels like it's all finally happening. Some of the sign confuses him and I internally scold myself for not bringing some other form of communication, maybe I need to bring a notepad and pen with me next time, I really must think ahead in these situations.

We pass a man in a shirt and formal trousers, tucked in at the waist with a belt and smart shoes on. He greets us formally, avoiding eye contact and swinging his arms at a swift pace. Jack greets him in return and when he's out of earshot, whispers to me.

"Do you think he's autistic?" It's a question he's asked previously because there is an autism residential unit by our house. I know it is Jack's intention to learn more about autism and so I give him a look to advise this is an inappropriate question. I've told him many times that autism doesn't have a specific look but that doesn't stop him from asking my opinion on the potential of other's neurotypes, something that I don't like to comment on. He knows now that some things he says are offensive, like the vast majority of people he's not educated in autism, but he's eager to learn and for that reason I communicate: 'no I'm not a human autism detector" by moving my hand in a wave across my body before emulating a scan over his body. He laughs in response, and I can't help but return a wide smile, it feels so good to be able to engage in humour through sign, I feel like I'm really getting the hang of this.

Enjoying the experience, I gesture a penis on top of my head as 'dickhead' and again mime a body scan over him. In response he makes a beeping noise and we both collapse into fits of laughter. We return to the house hand in hand, where I spend the remainder of the evening in silence, smiling at Jack and cuddling him to communicate my fondness of spending some silent time with him.

It's not always easy, like this, there are times when we really misunderstand each other, and we argue. Often Jack bears witness to my meltdowns, which he's learnt through experience not to continue to argue during this time. For many years, he's followed me around the house, seeking to close the argument by getting his point across only for me to scream at him, cover my ears, close my eyes and slam doors in his face. All of that we see now was an attempt to escape the situation because processing the language was too much for my brain and I couldn't regulate my emotions.

When we first entered the Coronavirus lockdown we rented a tiny house with only four rooms, a kitchen, bathroom, bedroom and living room and we were thrown into spending every second of the day together in close proximity. The first few months were hard, and we argued constantly, making us question if we should really have moved in together. In that house there was no escape from the argument and the law stated you could only leave the house for exercise once a day, so any argument we could hear each other arguing back in the next room.

I remember feeling utterly trapped, unable to escape from the words Jack spoke and the feelings of distress whenever we butted heads. I would scream at him when the argument got too much and attempt to leave the room only for him to call after me that I 'always run away' whenever there's conflict and I was 'being a child'. I would scream more, my head filled with a fog that I could not filter or process my thoughts and words would fly out that I didn't mean, making him angrier, his words came quicker and in harsher tones. I would often run away and hide in the covers of our bed, Jack would follow, telling me that I needed to act like an adult and confront the argument. I didn't have the words to verbalise what I wanted to say and whenever I tried, they always missed the mark. He would ask me for evidence or to return back to the cause of the argument and I wouldn't have access to my memories or be able to understand the concept of time and quantity in those moments.

Not being able to explain myself like this would wind me up further until I was screaming, crying and wailing, tearing at my hair and pressing my nails into my skin. It was in those moments that Jack thought I'd completely lost it, asking me why I was behaving in such a way and why my emotions were completely disproportionate to the situation. Those questions brought flashbacks of previous experiences and the whole thing escalated until Jack became horrified by what he saw and left the room.

It is only now that we can appreciate these moments as autistic meltdowns, where I need to be given space, time to process and met with calm rather than chaos. I often reflect that if my mum had known this earlier in my life things would have been a whole lot different. Because my mum is very alike to me, our emotions would pin-ball off each other and we would become a ball of dysregulation, unable to soothe ourselves or the other one until my calm and somewhat, scared dad came home from work to manage the situation and regulate both of us. Back then, and even now I hold so much shame about those meltdowns because everyone always saw what they thought was a disproportionate reaction to the situation and I would be labelled a drama queen or psychotic.

I hate knowing that ex-boyfriends have witness me in my worst states, unable to breathe through crying and screaming and tearing at my clothes and skin. I hate what they will have seen and what they will have thought in response. I hate that Jack has seen that part, but it is part of me, and he wouldn't know me if he hadn't experienced those moments.

Since my diagnosis and since Jack and I sat down and had a calm conversation about how to manage conflicts in our relationship, I haven't had a single meltdown of that propensity. He allows me to walk off from the situation and re-join the conversation when my emotions are more stable. He knows that I can't process what he's saying or articulate myself well enough, so he knows not to bother, and he accepts written communication for me to explain my thoughts and feelings. Don't get me wrong, he certainly isn't allowing me to act however I please but he's understanding of my reactivity and that things need to be different for me to manage it. Without us clearly communicating what we both needed from the other we certainly wouldn't have made it work but I'll forever be grateful that we did.

29
THE END OF HARRY

2007

High school seems daunting as it approaches, there's only two weeks left, and I've nearly perfected my new mask. I'm going to change my name to Haz and introduce myself to everyone that way, when the teachers call me Harry, I'll correct them, because I won't be Harry anymore. I'm extremely nervous about school but I'm also super excited because it's a chance for me to reinvent myself and start from scratch. I'm no longer going to be known as the girl who weed on stage or said silly things in class or played childish games on the playground. Peter wants to stay in touch when we leave Sunflowers, but I don't know how to do that if I'm not going to be Harry anymore. I think I need to leave all of Harry's friends behind to make this successful, just like all the things that Harry likes and believes in and that makes me a bit sad but it's all for the best.

This summer, I've not seen my school friends because I need to put distance between the Harry I am when I'm with them and the person I'm going to become at my new school. There are also the people at tennis going to my high school that I'm going to have to fool into thinking I'm a new person because I can't change tennis clubs too, that's too much change. I'm going to have to continue to be called Harry at tennis and that's going to be confusing, but I mustn't slip into old habits. Immogen from tennis will be at my new school so she'll be able to report back to them all that I'm cool now, and they'll all start to invite me to practice.

Of course, I'll still be friends with Anna but that's easy because she likes me just the way that I am, and I don't have to pretend so much around her. I need to be different around my family though, I've been driving mum and dad up the wall this summer, making them shout at me and Beth keeps reminding me that I'm going to be the death of my mother with all that shouting I'm making her do. I still don't know what that means but it doesn't look good because she had an angry face, and she shook her head at me. I need to be better for mum and dad, so Haz will be a better daughter as well as a more popular girl. Maybe if I start to make more friends and try harder to fit in mum and dad will like me better anyway, mum's always asking me to try and find people to play tennis with and have over to play. I think it would make her happy if I spent less time on my own or with her and more time with lots of friends.

Last week, mum asked me if she'd like me to drive us up to school now and again to get me used to the drive to school but I said no, next time I go I need to be Haz and I haven't fine-tuned the mask yet. Anyway, I will be going on a school bus so it will be totally different than going in the car. I begged mum and dad not to put me on a bus because the drive to places is always my time to not speak and cope with my anxiety, planning what I'm going to do and say and who I will be in that situation. But they can't take me to school every day because mum is going back to work full time and it would take two hours out of her working days. This means that I'll have less time to put my mask on and get into character, which is frustrating.

I think I worry most about the bus because it's going to be noisy and have lots of people on it that I don't know. At least at school there's a seating plan and I don't have to decide where to sit or wait for someone to say it's okay for me to sit next to them. Linda's going to be on my bus, and I really hope that she'll save me a seat. Dad said that her parents are going to drop her and her brother off at our bus stop across the road, rather than the one nearer her house so that I'll have someone to talk to and get on the bus with. This made me feel a little better, but then it means even less time to get into my mask and be Haz. Everything is very confusing about going to big school and I'm a mixture of feelings, some that I like and some that I don't.

I really wish that I could continue to be Harry because it's so much easier when I don't have to think about the way I'm acting, how my face looks and what I say but no one seems to like me when I'm myself. It seems to make everyone happier and less stressed when I try harder to be like everyone else, so that's what I must do to make sure everyone is happy with me at my new school. I might as well not have had my ear operation if I'm just going to be myself and weird, I need to pin back my personality like they did to my ears. No one would ever know that my ears used to look different from everyone else's so maybe then it will be the same for my personality, maybe people will only be able to see the little cracks if they get up close and I point it out.

Sometimes, I point out the things that are weird about me, like my webbed toes or my ears, just to fill the gaps in a conversation and it seems to make people interested in me. I also really like that I have different things to other people, when people ask me to describe myself that bit always seems easier to describe than what I like and who I am, because that's a really hard question to answer. I need to stop telling people about my quirks at my new school because then people will find out that I was weird in my old school, and I need them to think that everything about me is normal.

I've changed my hair for new school too, Linda always said that she didn't like the curls in her hair and my hair is always so much curlier than everyone else's so I've pinned it back, just like my ears so that no one can tell how curly it is. I really like it when my hair is out of my face, and it makes me less moody because sometimes my hair tickles my face in a certain way and it makes my whole body feel wrong and like it will explode. Mum asked me if I wanted her to style my new hair, because she says it looks 'severe' but this is how I wear it for tennis and so do all the other girls at the tennis club so it should help me fit in. It feels weird to change all of these things but all I have to remind myself is that if I just try harder then everyone will like me and I will fit in, not stand out.

I think about the glittery, platforms I saw in the charity shop so long ago with Anna and her mum. I'm so glad now that Kim didn't buy them for me because they would only have set me apart from everyone else that little bit more and it isn't safe to be myself and wear the things that make me look different. I've learnt that if I'm going to succeed at high school I can't wear bold shoes, I have to be a lesser version of me and be more like the cool girls I see on TV. So maybe if I had those shoes now, I would throw them in the bin, along with all of the other things I own that no one else would wear or play with. My first day of school tomorrow is going to be great because today is the last day of being Harry, everyone will only know Haz from now on.

30
IT WAS RIGHT IN FRONT OF ME ALL ALONG

April 2022

It's Sunday, which means it's food shop day. Usually, Jack and I visit Tesco together and he does all the talking to strangers, whilst I focus on organising the shopping list and packing the food into specific bags. To anyone else, Jack might look unhelpful, standing around whilst I unpack the food onto the till, then packing it into bags without his assistance, but he helps with the communication. He would only get in the way of my specific packing system if he tried to help.

Today is different; Jack is with his family so the food shop is down to me, triggering a new phase of complete silence. At times like this, I don't even want to listen to music in the car because my brain is too busy preparing for what being at the shop is going to be like. Just a few weeks back they had changed the whole aisle system in the shop, with some of my safe foods, like tacos, no longer being in the same place. It was an overwhelming nightmare where I got very stressed, I only manage to complete a shop without meltdowns if I know the layout of the shop and where all my usual foods are. I still haven't got used to where everything is in the shop so going on my own today feels like a big task.

Over-stimulation threatens me as soon as I enter the building, the smells, lights and sounds are almost too much to bear. To distract myself I look down at the paper list in my hand and reset myself into shopping mode, *if I just focus on the task all will be okay*, I remind myself silently. I collect my usual vegetables from the first two aisles, it's always the same so I don't need to refer to my list as much. Next is the meat aisle, just chicken sausages, chicken breast and turkey, that's it, not a stressful aisle. But next on the list is the newly arranged taco aisle, clumsily I scan the shelves for the chicken stock, my eyes jumping from one item to another without no systematic process, it's a mess. It's then, out of the corner of my eye that I notice a little boy stood rigidly, just a few feet away. I recognise him immediately.

Ben is a little, blond-haired boy with the most innocent face, his hair frequently flops into his face. He hates having his hair cut so it's always extra-long. He's got his favourite teddy in his hand, a floppy-eared, grey bunny, the epitome of 'ultimate softness'. So unlike Scruffy in appearance, but similar in so many ways, he's something that could never be parted from Ben because of his meaning to him. Ben loves ice-lollies, dogs and ball pits, he hates bright sunlight, sticky things on his hands and loud noises. I know all this because I've known Ben since he was a little baby, I've also experienced the world in the same way as him because he is also autistic.

I approach him with a wide smile but unlike most times, it is not reciprocated. His mother turns as I approach and matches my smile, wide-eyed and happy to see me again.

"Harry, it's so good to see you!" She bellows, always a

loud talker, so much so that both Ben and I wince slightly. Such a slight change in our body postures that's almost undetectable by the untrained eye, though we both acknowledge it in each other. We catch up about what we've both been doing since we last met and she tells me all about how Ben is doing at his new school, he's now in year five of primary school. Ben looks on but doesn't engage in the conversation, though he holds my gaze throughout, eager to hear what I'm saying.

"I'm so happy to see you, buddy!" I say as I lean down to his level, his mouth twitches at the side into the slightest smile. I can tell he's happy to see me but he's not happy in his current situation. "What are you excited to eat when you get home?" He shrugs and points to me, I know immediately what this means.

"Me? Well, I'm having tacos tonight." I gesture to the tacos in my shopping trolley, "It's my most *favourite* food and I would eat it every, single day if I could but my boyfriend gets really bored with eating chicken tacos every night!" He starts to giggle, covering his mouth as the sound escapes.

"You struggle to speak sometimes don't you, Ben?" His mum explains, though I know this already.

"Well, we've spoke about how I find it difficult to use my voice when I get nervous, haven't we? Most of the time it's when I'm in the supermarket because everything is just so overwhelming." Ben looks from his mum to me, looking purposefully into my eyes and raises his hand in a gesture for me to meet it with my own, our palms touch and he curls his fingers around mine. He doesn't have to use his words, this communicates everything that needs to be said 'you understand me, you get me, thank you,' It takes everything in me not to cry with overwhelming happiness but instead I smile back at him and allow him to hold onto my hand for as long as he needs to feel connected to another neurodivergent person.

I can't change the trauma I experienced as an undiagnosed, neurodivergent child, I can't rewrite my story or support the younger version of me. I can't change the extreme low points in my life or prevent all of my loved ones being touched by them, nor would I. Those experiences have made me who I am today and where I am now, I certainly wouldn't be the person I am proud to be. What I do know, is that my experiences, my words and my passion can change the futures of other neurodivergent children, those who are experiencing such similar things and I'll continue to fight for better circumstances for them for as long as I need to.

Ben's mum looks at me with tears welling in her eyes and I decide to give her some time to recompose herself in the middle of the busy shop. I tell Ben how the pesky supermarket workers have moved all the ingredients in this aisle, and it's made me really stressed. He eagerly agrees to help me look for the chicken stock, with me showing him a picture of what I'm looking for and is thrilled when he finally spots it on the shelf above him. He looks at me expectantly, throwing his finger up in the air towards the item and smiling, wildly. *I've found it for you!* I can almost hear him say without words.

"Ahh, you superstar!" I praise him, offering a high-five as he often has to me. "I'm so proud of you, what a great way to tell me you'd found it." Ben knows he doesn't have to use his voice with me, when he's overwhelmed, we can always play silent games and make each other giggle with gestures and facial expressions.

As I pack the shopping into the car boot at the end of a fulfilling shop experience, I look down at my hands and for the first time notice the outline of an infinity symbol in the ring on my right, ring finger. I was gifted the ring from my mum, passed down as a family heirloom from her grandparents, I'd always seen the letter "S" in the ring. But looking at it now, the shape is as clear as day: the sign for neurodiversity. Just like my autism and ADHD, it had been there all along but only now was I ready to see it, embrace it and let it guide the new journey I have ahead.

31
WHAT I WISH YOU KNEW

Hey Little Harry, Big Harry here. I thought I would write you a letter of all the things I wish that you knew, because I know how much you love words and writing letters, I guess we have that in common.

I want you to know that you will spend most of your life knowing that there is something different about you, but not being able to put your finger on it. It's not hard to realise that everyone else is experiencing the world in a different way and not with as much adversity. You'll spend much of your life trying to be someone you're not, constantly adapting your persona to fit the situation, but I wish you knew that the person underneath the mask is better than anyone you could ever pretend to be.

I'm really sorry that you lose parts of yourself along your journey and learn that it isn't safe to be who you want and need to be. I'm trying so hard to get back to being just like you, Harry. Everything about you is what I wish I could be now: fearless, unapologetic, eccentric and completely individual. Please figure out what makes you happy and not everyone else, you deserve to put yourself first for a while and connect with what makes you tick. I'm sorry that your voice wasn't heard or listened to by enough people over the years, there are many, many people that I can't begin to count that have let you down and failed you.

I wish you knew not to listen to other people when they invalidate your feelings, experiences and thoughts. You support yourself to process everything you're thinking and feeling just by writing it down and reading it back, never lose touch with words, Harry, they are your saving grace.

I'm sorry that the autism diagnostic criteria is male favouring and your diagnosis got missed time and time again by the professionals who were supposed to keep you safe and healthy. I wish I could take away the pain of not being able to make your needs known and to access other ways of communicating, which could have prevented so much anguish. I'm sorry that at twenty-six you're only just beginning to stop forcing yourself to speak to people when every bone in your body tells you that you can't.

I wish you'd have known that you had every right to make your own decisions, no matter how upset you were or when you couldn't speak. You should never have felt like you had to ask for everyone else's opinions before you could decide even the smallest thing. You deserved better.

I wish you knew that you were neurodivergent, so, so long ago when it would have made you feel accepting of the support you needed so badly. I wish other people had known you were neurodivergent so that they wouldn't have imposed so much strain on your mental health by asking you to be something that you weren't. Maybe then you would have felt less shame and responsibility for the strain it put on your family. Maybe, just maybe you would have been happier.

There will be people along the way, who misinterpret your communication and intentions, friends that fall out with you because they don't understand why you do things the way you do. Through it all, you've made some incredible friendships that I know will last a lifetime. And with that, you should thank Linda, who has always been there for you throughout childhood and into adulthood, always being the strongest person you know and always backs you, no matter what. Your great friend, Naomi, who you have yet to meet. She is that person that just gets you, I can't wait for you to meet her, Harry. Naomi has helped you to reach your dreams of being an author and is the most talented artist, you're so very lucky to have her in your life.

Of course, you'd never have got very far if it wasn't for mum and dad, there's no two people in the world who could have made your life more complete. They are everything that parents should be and more, their support and love will never falter, you can count on that. No matter what you threw at them along the way, they've always been your biggest advocates and fans, there are no words in the world that could explain your love for them, especially now. I wish you knew how much they love you and wouldn't change you for the world, no matter what. Alex, as well, who was the first person who really understood you and taught you that it was more than okay to be who you are, that it's cool to enjoy boys' toys and clothes. Though you will be further apart in distance, your bond won't change; he will always be your favourite person.

And then there's Jack. Sometimes in life you just meet the right person, at the right time and you know there and then that you'll spend the rest of your life with them. You'll want to throw things at his head most days because he's just so frustrating, but he hears you even when you don't speak, loves you for your quirks, not despite them, whilst firmly putting you in your place. Jack is the type of man that every person is lucky to have met, he's come into your life and taught you the most important lesson of all – how to love yourself and seek happiness from within. Although you will never want to experience life without him, he's taught you how to.

Most of all, I wish you knew just how great you are, Harry. You are a little girl with such a big heart, who always wanted to make other people smile and happy with your unique sense of humour. I know you don't see it now, but you are infinitely strong and kind. You are unique and wild and immensely powerful. The resilience you have is unequivocal, being moulded, excluded and chastised when you should have been allowed to be yourself, is something I could not go back and do again. I hope you know that I will forever be proud of who you made me become.

But your story is not told you have so much still to say and changes to evoke. Your words have always been your power, ever since you wrote those childhood stories that got hung on the wall. All of the lyrics you used to write to cope with the emotions that built up inside were important, you've always had something to say and now you've found your voice. Speak up, Harry because it's time that people started to listen.

ABOUT THE AUTHOR

Hat is a neurodivergent Speech & Language Therapist, autism assessor, public speaker, podcaster and blogger. She runs the Instagram account @hat.talks.uk and creates content to support the acceptance and celebration of neurodivergence. On her website, Hat has developed The Post-Diagnosis Handbook for Autistic People, and The ADHD Handbook, to support people's understanding of autism and ADHD. She was identified as autistic in 2022, at the age of 26 and shortly after self-identified as an ADHDer. Outside of work, Hat is dog mum to Meeno, an Assistance Dog in Training and lives with her partner in West Yorkshire.

www.hattalks.uk

Printed in Great Britain
by Amazon